COMBAT FAITH

Books by Hal Lindsey

The Late Great Planet Earth

Satan Is Alive and Well on Planet Earth

There's a New World Coming

The Liberation of Planet Earth

The Terminal Generation

The 1980s: Countdown to Armageddon

The Promise

The Rapture: Truth or Consequences

Combat Faith

A Prophetical Walk
Through the Holy Land

COMBAT FAITH

Hal Lindsey

BANTAM BOOKS
TORONTO · NEW YORK · LONDON · SYDNEY · AUCKLAND

COMBAT FAITH

A Bantam Book / September 1986

Library of Congress Cataloging-in-Publication Data

Lindsey, Hal.
  Combat faith.

  1. Faith.   I. Title.
  BT771.2.L56   1986   234'.2   86-10746
  ISBN 0-553-34342-4

Book design by Nicola Mazzella.

Published simultaneously in the United States and Canada

PRINTED IN THE UNITED STATES OF AMERICA

S   11   10 9   8   7

I dedicate this book to my true and faithful friend, Dotty Larson, who was faithful to pray for me in my most difficult hours and continually spoke the truth to me in love. She is a woman of God whose life is an example of combat faith. May her reward be great.

Contents

ing of the Spirit • The Filling of the Spirit and Spiritual
Gifts • The Filling of the Spirit and Maturity • The Filling of
the Spirit Is Not a Mutual Assistance Program • Why the Be-
liever Can Never Be Condemned • Two Principles of Life
Contrasted • How to Be Filled With the Spirit • The War
Against the Devil • Our Strength • Intelligence Report on
Our Enemy • Checking Out Our Armor • The Belt of
Truth • The Breastplate • The Shoes • The Shield • The
Helmet • Our Sword • Prayer, Our Heavy Artillery • Having
Prepared, Be Ready to Fight! • Combating the World-
System • The Battle for Our Affections • Worldliness De-
fined • The Delicate Line • Final Briefing

Book of Remembrance • Kings and Priests • Higher Than Angels • We Shall Know God as He Now Knows Us • Hope, the Key to a Dynamic Present Faith

CHAPTER ONE

Hope for
the Gathering Storm

> But mark this: There will be terrible times in the last days. . . . The Spirit clearly says that in later times some will abandon the faith and follow deceiving spirits and things taught by demons.
>
> 2 Timothy 3:1 and 1 Timothy 4:1

Everyone was excited to begin. They were especially looking forward to the reading of a new section of the Gospel of Luke that had just been received from a secret home church in another city of the Soviet Union. Since Bibles are so scarce, the churches take them apart and exchange pages with each other.

It had taken all day for the local body of Christians to assemble. They had to come at different intervals in groups of two or at most three at a time so as not to attract the attention of the ever present KGB informers.

Just as they were about to sing with subdued volume (but not enthusiasm) their first hymn of praise, the door burst open and two Soviet soldiers with automatic weapons at the ready rushed in. They ordered everyone to line up against the far wall. "Anyone who will renounce faith in Jesus Christ may leave now. The rest of you remain with your hands up!" shouted one of the soldiers.

Two, then four, left. The soldiers said again in an even more threatening voice, "This is your last chance to renounce faith in Jesus Christ, or else face the consequences." The parents with children looked down reassuringly at their frightened little faces, but no one else left.

One of the soldiers walked over and slammed the door shut. Then they both put down their weapons and said, "Keep your hands up, but in praise to our Lord Jesus Christ, brothers." As the believers looked at them in total astonishment, the soldiers continued, "We have become believers through contact with other believers from home churches like yours. We were sent to arrest them, and instead were converted to their faith. But through our previous experiences, we learned that no one can be trusted unless he is willing to die for his faith."

(This is a true incident reported by the underground church in Russia.)

WILL THE CHURCH GO THROUGH A GREAT PERSECUTION?

Many Christians in the United States ask me if I think the Church will see the persecution before the beginning of the Tribulation (a seven-year period of worldwide catastrophe that immediately precedes the Second Coming of Christ). My answer is that according to recent estimates three fourths of the Church is *already* under severe persecution around the globe at this very moment. So it's really not a matter of whether there will be a severe persecution of the true Church, but whether it will hit the Church in the United States. In my perception of prophecy and current events, it definitely will.

Few Dare Call It Conspiracy!

There are many sources of persecution for the true Church today that are beginning to set the stage for the predicted great final assault against the people of God. However, there is an invisible hand behind all these forces, coordinating them into a virulent and lethal threat to believers worldwide,

2

that is too frequently not recognized. That mastermind is none other than the age-old enemy of God's children, Satan himself.

Satan, who is also called by the Scriptures the Devil, the Ruler of this world system, the Prince of the power of the atmosphere, and so on, is the most powerful and intelligent creature God ever created. He is the real source of the persecutions that are spreading over the world. The Bible indicates that shortly before the beginning of the Tribulation, the Lord will gradually remove His restraint of Satan and allow him to exercise his powers to set the stage for the unveiling of his masterpiece, the Antichrist.

Satan has virtually achieved most of the goals necessary to set the stage for the Antichrist's appearance.

Satan's most important goal in this regard is to destroy faith in the Bible as being the inerrant Word of God in the original autographs. This is important to him because apart from an inerrant Bible there is no way to know anything for sure. Without an infallible Bible there is no certain authority for discerning errors in doctrine or practices, or for identifying and exposing satanically produced supernaturalism. If the Bible contains errors, then who is to say where and what these errors are. Each person could claim the Bible to be in error in those particular verses that contradict his prejudices and pet sins.

Satan has been enormously successful in his assault against the Bible's inerrancy. Beginning with the so-called Higher Critical school of thought of the nineteenth-century state-supported seminaries in Germany, the Bible's accepted inerrancy began to be subjected to an all out attack. Without hard historical evidence, these schools began to construct very clever and supposedly scholarly arguments against the Bible's authenticity, which were based entirely upon subjective arguments. Unbelief, and the justification thereof, always finds ready ears, especially in the academic field. So the blatant heretical teachings of the German schools soon spread to the seminaries of the United Kingdom and the United States.

How successfully has this heresy been spread in America? Among the traditional mainline denominations of Christendom in the United States, only the Southern Baptist and the

Missouri Synod of the Lutheran churches officially still hold to an unqualified belief in biblical inerrancy, [and the Southern Baptists are involved in a furious civil war over the subject.] Some individual pastors and members of the other various denominations may still believe in the Scripture's verbal inspiration, but officially the hierarchies reject it. Those who today officially hold to an unqualified Divine inspiration of the Bible are found mostly in the nondenominational church movements.

One of the most misleading falsehoods that these unbelieving self-proclaimed scholars of the Bible have been able to sell the general public is that one cannot be a "scholar" or an "intellectual" and still believe in the inerrancy of the Scriptures. Typical of this kind of arrogant thinking is the following statement:

> New Testament scholarship today agrees that Jesus of Nazareth was baptized by John the Baptist, that as a teacher and healer Jesus attracted disciples, and that he was executed by crucifixion. But the chairman of Stanford University's religious studies department says the progress of biblical research has made anything else historically questionable.
>
> "So far as the biblical historian is concerned there is scarcely a popularly held traditional belief about Jesus that is not regarded with considerable skepticism," says Stanford's Van Harvey.
>
> The "enormous gap" continues between what the average lay person believes to be true about Jesus and what "the great majority of New Testament scholars" conclude after 150 years of research and debate, he said.
>
> The Stanford professor said that New Testament scholarship has become so specialized and requires so much preparation that many scholars feel "the lay person has simply been disqualified from having any right to a judgement regarding the truth or falsity of certain historical claims. . . . This conclusion, which initially sounds so outrageous and arrogant, is really nothing more than the extension of the attitudes of

the scholarly community to its own fledgling members," he said.[1]

This sort of heretical teaching is typical of what is being taught our children concerning the Bible in universities across the country. If a student believes in the historical truths of Christianity today, he is in for withering ridicule and low grades. I can say this with authority because I was a missionary for fifteen years on the college campuses of America, ministering on more than 150 university and college campuses.

The attitude of these professors should not be surprising, because the Scriptures warned, **"The man without the Spirit does not accept the things that come from the Spirit of God, for they are foolishness to him, and he cannot understand them, because they are spiritually discerned."** (1 Corinthians 2:14) The most educated man who has not been born spiritually is completely unable to discern the meaning of the Scriptures. The reason is not a lack of intelligence, but a lack of the right kind of life with which to perceive the biblical truths. So for these self-proclaimed scholars to say that the average lay person is not qualified to judge what is true or false in the Bible is the epitome of vain pride and exaltation of human wisdom in defiance of God.

This is exactly the kind of situation the Bible predicted would come in the last days of the Church on earth. When the Lord Jesus predicted the birth pangs that would signal His imminent return, the only signs He repeated were the rise of false messiahs, false prophets, satanically produced signs, wonders and miracles (which would counterfeit those produced by the Holy Spirit), and false doctrines. Three times He warned us not to be deceived by them (Matthew 24:4–5, 11, 24).

Just before the apostle Peter was crucified upside down, he dashed off his second epistle in which he warned about of the same things:

But there were . . . false prophets among the people, just as there will be false teachers among you. They will secretly introduce destructive heresies, even denying the sovereign LORD Who bought them—

bringing swift destruction on themselves. Many will follow their shameful ways and will bring the WAY OF TRUTH* [the Bible] into disrepute. (2 Peter 2:1–2)

Peter warned us of these things right after he made one of the strongest points of his life. He declared that what the Bible says about the Second Coming of Christ is more sure than what he had heard with his ears and had seen with his own eyes. He based that testimony on the incredible experience he had with the Lord Jesus on the Mount of Transfiguration, where he heard God the Father speak and saw the Lord Jesus as He will appear in radiant glory at His Second Coming.

Peter gave the reason for the Bible being more sure than our experiences and emotions:

Above all, you must understand that no prophecy of Scripture came about by the prophet's own interpretation. For prophecy never had its origin in the will of man, but men spoke from God as they were carried along by the Holy Spirit. (2 Peter 1:20–21)

The apostle Paul also prophesied this same sort of warning to the latter day church just before he was put to death:

All Scripture is God-breathed and is useful for teaching, rebuking, correcting and training in righteousness, so that the man of God may be thoroughly equipped for every good work.
    In the presence of God and of Christ Jesus, who will judge the living and the dead, and in view of His appearing and His kingdom, I give you this charge: Preach the Word; be prepared [when it is convenient and when it is not]; correct, rebuke and encourage—with great patience and careful instruc-

---

*Throughout the book, my emphases in quotes from Scripture are shown by ALL CAPS or *boldface italics;* and amplified word or phrase meanings are set off by square [ ] brackets.

6

tion. For the time will come when men will not put up with sound doctrine. Instead, to suit their own desires, they will gather around them a great number of teachers to say what their itching ears want to hear. They will turn their ears away from the TRUTH [the Bible] and turn aside to myths. (2 Timothy 3:16–4:4 HL)

Paul identified the historical time to which this prophecy applies at the beginning of the context: "But mark this: There will be TERRIBLE TIMES in the last days [of the Church]. . . ." (2 Timothy 3:1) We are at the beginning of those "terrible times." But thank God that He has provided us with full equipment for inner peace, stability, and victory in the midst of them!

THE ADVENT OF AN AGE OF PARANORMAL

Another goal Satan has almost completed is to bring the world at large to accept supernaturalism through the occult and false religions. Satan loves religion as long as it takes one away from the Truth about the Lord Jesus Christ. His goal has never been to have a nonreligious world that rejected the supernatural.

Though Satan delights to use atheistic philosophies and political movements like communism to further his purposes, his ultimate purpose is to bring about a religious world that believes in the supernatural so that it will accept and worship him through his ruler, the Antichrist, whom he will personally indwell.

The Bible predicts that the Antichrist will perform all kinds of false miracles and supernatural phenomena in the last days in order to lead mankind to worship and follow Satan. So the world will have to be conditioned beforehand to accept counterfeit miracles.

Jesus Christ warned that there would be an explosion of satanic miracles in the era leading to His return:

For false Christs and false prophets will appear and perform great signs and miracles to deceive even the

7

elect—if that were possible. See, I have told you ahead of time. (Matthew 24:24–25)

Paul predicted the same thing:

The coming of the Lawless One [the Antichrist] will be in accordance with the work of Satan displayed in all kinds of counterfeit miracles, signs and wonders, and in every sort of evil that deceives those who are perishing. They perish because they refused to love [and accept] the TRUTH [the Bible] and so be saved. (2 Thessalonians 2:9–10)

This current situation wherein the world has been prepared for Satan's counterfeit miracles was cleverly set up over the last two hundred years. During the age of rationalism, which generally began in the eighteenth century and extended through the early twentieth century, man was gradually conditioned to reject supernatural phenomena through the ascendancy of a false application of science and its dogmatic pronouncements.

But when the Devil had destroyed general acceptance of the Bible, he switched his tactics. Satan began to bring about an unprecedented revival of the occult, which accelerated in the mid sixties. Now we have former atheists who believe in the supernatural, which they have labeled "extrasensory perception and paranormal phenomena." Many major universities today have a department that specializes in this field. Surprisingly, the Soviet Union has experimented in the "paranormal field" more extensively than any other nation. They believe that there are possible military applications for extrasensory perception. This atheistic government believes that ESP is a kind of extension of the latent powers of the human soul.

Without the Bible as a guide, man has no way to discern whether supernatural phenomena are produced by some imagined mysterious latent power of the human soul, or by Satan through the occult, or by the miraculous power of God.

I believe that it is through the sphere of the occult and religious deceptions that Satan will orchestrate the greatest persecution of believers in history. The occult is part of a coordinated conspiracy that is determined to bring about a one-world religion, and the true Christian is the greatest obstacle to that goal.

I believe some of this will hit *all* of the true Churches before they are snatched out of the world in the Rapture. But the greatest massacre will fall on those who become believers in Jesus as Messiah during the seven-year Tribulation after the Church is gone. A multitude too great to be numbered will be martyred by a one-world religious system, which will be led by the Antichrist during that dreadful period (Revelation 7:9–17).

The Dawning of the "New Age Movement"

Many factors are already working together to set up this one-world religion, but the most powerful of these is called the New Age Movement. This is a movement that touches so many areas of life with so many kinds of deception that it almost defies definition. Yet there are definite unifying factors that combine to make this one of the most deceptive and dangerous threats the Christian faith has ever encountered. Only the Devil could coordinate such a vast divergence of interests, views, and religions into a cohesive movement.[2]

The movement grew out of the disillusionment that resulted from the idealism and desire for total commitment of the 1960s.

Although the "Jesus people" movement was one of the results of that longing, counterfeit forms of religion and left-wing political organizations also captured this idealism and desire for some form of total commitment. Most people of that area "burned out" and were disillusioned after counterfeit religions such as the Children of God and the Hare Krishnas proved to be unworthy of such commitment. In the same way, the left-wing political movements, with their frequent calls for Marxist-style violence (which didn't fit the pacifistic ideals of most of the "flower children" generation) were left without a rallying cause after the Vietnam War ended.

The Religious Invasion from the East

Into this spiritual vacuum came the New Age Movement with a compromise to fit everyone's needs. The New Age supplies a form of universal religion to satisfy the quest for spiritual fulfillment left over from the sixties. The "new truth" calls for us to: look inside ourselves and find "the god within"; discover the common energy that makes us one with animals, nature, and the universe; and unleash through various forms of meditation the "unlimited human potential" that supposedly flows from this inner universal force.

To those familiar with Eastern religion, particularly Hinduism, this should sound very familiar. The gurus of India have had a major role in spawning the New Age thinking. They offered to a guilt-ridden, drug and free-sex generation a religion that negated sin and required no moral commitment. The New Age teaches that God is an impersonal force that has both a good side and an evil side, and that we ourselves are gods because this "divine force" dwells within us all.

These doctrines remove any belief in a personal creator God who exists apart from the things He has created. They also blind us to our sin, need for a Savior, and the special uniqueness and value of each individual human being.

The New Age has taken many different pursuits and turned them into a kind of "religion smorgasbord" that attempts to fill the sense of religious hunger and need for spiritual fulfillment in us all.

The New Age "Diets"

For example: Diets have been turned into a religion in this sense. The Hindu idea of reincarnation and the oneness of mankind and animals have produced a religious vegetarianism. As I walked down a London street today, I saw that "Murderers!" had been written on the window of a butcher shop by a new kind of militant vegetarian group. On the cover of a recent rock album I saw, "To eat meat is to murder!"

There is nothing wrong with forsaking meat eating if

that's your thing. But if it is made into an aggressive religious crusade, it is wrong. God gave certain animals as food for all mankind. He also gave man dominion over the animals and all the earth. Animals were made for man, not man for animals (Acts 10:10–16; Genesis 1:28; I Tim. 4:3–4). Some Eastern-styled religions show more concern and compassion for animals than they do for humans.

The New Age and Physical Fitness

Exercise has also been exploited by the New Age. Yoga, and the inseparable religious concepts that go with it, have found devout followers. It has been fitted into the overall religious umbrella of the New Age Movement.

Various forms of Hindu meditation and yoga exercises have been made part of many public-school curricula under the guise of being a "nonreligious" way of discovering your "human potential." This is New Age thinking to the core. There is no such thing as nonreligious transcendental meditation. The "personal mantras" given to be chanted during the so-called neutral, nonreligious transcendental meditation practice are all names of Eastern demon gods and are intended to be used in worship and invocations to them.

The New Age Invasion of Education

It is frightening to observe that our government-supported public schools have become the number-one target of the New Age "evangelistic" efforts toward a one-world religion and government.

This is clearly spelled out in an article by John Dunphy in the *Humanist* magazine:

I am convinced that the battle for humankind's future must be waged and won in the public school class-room by teachers who correctly perceive their role as the proselytizers of a new faith: a religion of humanity that recognizes and respects the spark of what

11

theologians call divinity in every human being. These teachers must embody the same selfless dedication as the most rabid fundamentalist preachers, for they will be ministers of another sort, utilizing a classroom instead of a pulpit to convey humanist values in whatever subject they teach, regardless of the educational level—preschool, day care or large state university. The classroom must and will become an arena of conflict between the old and the new—the rotting corpse of Christianity, together with all its adjacent evils and misery, and the new faith of humanism, resplendent in its promise of a world in which the never-realized Christian ideal of "love thy neighbor" will finally be achieved.[3]

This is not an isolated expression of the New Age Movement's intentions. In another article concerning public education published in *New Age* magazine, educators Jack Canfield and Paula Klimek wrote,

In a growing number of classrooms throughout the world, education is beginning to move into a new dimension. More and more teachers are exposing children to *ways of contacting their inner wisdom and their higher selves*. . . . New Age education has arrived . . . *an influx of spiritual teachings from the East*, combined with new psychological perspective in the West, has resulted in a fresh look at the learning process—the distinction between knowledge and wisdom, the student/teacher relationship, *and the purpose of life*. . . . Within the last five years we have also witnessed the birth of "transpersonal education"—the acknowledgment of one's inner and spiritual dimensions—through working with such forms as dreams, *meditating, guided imagery,* biofeedback, centering, mandalas, and so forth.[4] [Emphases mine.]

The New Age recognizes the fundamental Christian as its archenemy and main obstacle. An article in the *Humanist* by educator Ron Miller brings this out:

Religious fundamentalism is not the only opponent of self-responsibility and creative thinking; so is a scientistic materialism which categorically rejects the human hunger for spiritual meaning. . . . Humanism must be an unceasing effort to unlock new meanings, to liberate repressed potential, to help the human species evolve to ever greater intellectual and moral and spiritual powers. *This should also be the purpose of education.*[5] [Emphases mine.]

Anyone who says that our public schools are religiously neutral is dangerously misinformed, or worse, is part of the deceptive process itself. While Christians slept, the New Age movement got control of our schools and now crams its views down our throats. Even if we send our children to a Christian private school, they seek [to force us to accept their "approved" curriculum and text books]. The New Agers are "tolerant" of everyone except those who hold to Biblical Christianity. Because of this, an inevitable persecution of true believers will come from this movement.

Their goals are, perhaps unwittingly, the same as those predicted for the Antichrist and his followers—a world that will worship a man and proclaim, **"Peace and security!"** and, **"Who is like the beast** (namely, the Antichrist who will be the World Ruler)**? Who is able to make war with him?"** (I Thessalonians 5:3 and Revelation 13:4 HL)

New Agers often use seminars purported to develop "Human Potential" and "Personal Growth" to lure people into their various religious cults.

The New Age and Visualization

Linked to meditation is another popular religious exercise called "visualization." A person is taught through various meditation techniques how to use his powers of imagination to visualize what he wants and then will it into existence. Devotees of these things say that "it works." (And it does up to a certain point.) It is kind of a "faith in faith" that mobilizes our human goal orientation. It grieves me, however, to observe that some believers have unwittingly adapted this ancient occult practice into Christianity. Though this technique may help to promote a positive attitude, it places the burden of success upon your ability to "visualize" and thereby mobilize your own human abilities to achieve a victorious Christian life. In speaking with several experts on the occult, including Johanna Michaelsen, Dave Hunt, and Caryl Matrisciana, I've found that some people have been opened up to strong demonic oppression by this practice. It is certainly not a neutral technique that can be divorced from its occultic origins and then Christianized.

Why use a technique that originated in and is part of the occult, when there is a far better way that is based on truth? The Bible teaches that the power of faith is in its object, not in the faith itself, much less in our imagination. Our positive attitude should come from Christ-confidence instead of a humanly produced self-confidence. Paul gives our correct model: **"I can do all things through Christ, who keeps on strengthening me."** (Philippians 4:13 HL)

The New Age and "Alternative Medicine"

What has been called traditional or alternative or holistic medicine is also used by the New Agers. This is a form of treatment that often works, but frequently does so primarily by the manipulation of occultic power. (For example, acupuncture is based on the aligning of the "Life Force," called *Chi*, a concept founded in Eastern mysticism.)

The New Age Movement has embraced and brought under its influence many other groups, such as environmental and ecology movements, antinuclear peace movements, group sensitivity movements, some forms of psychology, liberal Christian churches, animal rights groups, and so on. Many of the people involved in these various organizations may be sincere in their desire to protect the environment and help mankind. Nevertheless many of the organizations they have joined have ulterior motives that fit precisely into the New Age scenario.

The Coming Collision

A very real danger to true Biblical Christianity comes from the inevitable collision between it and the diametrically opposite doctrines of the New Age Movement. New Age objections to the teachings of Christianity are not new, but they have been cast into a new and vastly broader context.

New Agers believe that the Christian teaching of the existence of one true personal God, and faith in the Lord Jesus as the only way of salvation, is the height of bigotry and a threat to the progress of uniting the human family. They believe that the hope of mankind, indeed the only way to avert a nuclear holocaust and bring in world peace, is to unite all religions and bring in a one-world government. Any religion that hinders this larger goal is considered not only narrow minded and outmoded, but a threat to the very survival of the human race. In this new context of thinking are all the factors necessary to produce an all-out persecution of true Christians.

Benjamin Creme, the self-proclaimed "John the Baptist" of the New Age messiah called "Maitreya," clearly spells out what New Agers think about Jesus and Christianity:

People have been led to leave the churches in large numbers because the churches have presented a picture of the Christ impossible for the majority of thinking people today to accept—as the One and Only Son of God, sacrificed by His Loving Father to save Humanity from the results of its sins; as a blood sacrifice straight out of the old and outworn Jewish dispensation; as the unique revealer of God's nature . . . and as waiting in some mythical and unattractive Heaven until the end of the world, when He will return in a cloud of glory to the sound of Angels' trumpets, and, descending from those clouds, inherit His Kingdom.

The majority of thinking people today have rejected this view. . . . The view put forward by esotericism is surely more rational and acceptable and more in line with man's knowledge of history and science

15

and of religions *other than Christianity*.[6] [Emphasis mine.]

Alice A. Bailey, who is one of the leading prophetesses of the New Age Movement, gives a chilling plan for dealing with those who stand in opposition to the New Age program. In her book *The Externalisation of the Hierarchy* she details the "proper" use for the atomic bomb:

> It belongs to the United Nations for use (or let us rather hope, simply for threatened use) when aggressive action on the part of any nation rears its ugly head. It does not essentially matter whether that aggression is the gesture of any particular nation or group of nations or whether it is generated by the political groups of any powerful religious organization, such as the Church of Rome, who are as yet unable to leave politics alone and attend to the business for which all religions are responsible—leading human beings closer to the God of Love.[7]

According to this, most of the conservative Christian leaders in the United States would be nuked! I would suggest that those in the "peace movement" read carefully the writings on which their movement is founded.

THE COMMUNIST THREAT

A few years ago a pastor from behind the iron curtain shared with me the true incident I described at the beginning of this chapter. He told me about many terrible cases of persecution in the countries controlled by the communist system.

Communism is certainly one of the significant sources of persecution of the church in these last days. It is a philosophy that now controls approximately one third of the earth's population.

Faith is being tested by fire in those countries. According to a BBC special television report (April 1985), 33 percent of all prisoners in the vast Soviet prison system are "born-again

Christians," mostly from the Pentecostal and Baptist underground churches. This agrees with the observations of another former inmate of that system, Alexander Solzhenitsyn. His writings, which have challenged the moral weakness and lack of faith in Western civilization, reflect a faith that was born in the crucible of suffering. And yet his efforts to warn the West (particularly the churches) about the communist threat have mostly fallen upon deaf ears.

True Christians Are at Top of Communist Hit List

Wherever the communists take over, the first people to be imprisoned and/or executed are the born-again, Bible-believing Christians. In communist thinking these are unreformable people who cannot be converted to the "truth" of Marxist-Leninism.

There are hundreds of examples from all over the world of how Christians are persecuted by communists. One recent example concerning missionaries in Peru was reported in the January 1985 issue of the *Christian Inquirer*. Strangely, it was not reported in the secular media.

> Church groups including Food for the Hungry, the Mennonite Church and the National Evangelical Church in Peru are providing emergency funds to victims of escalating guerrilla warfare by a Marxist terrorist group in central Peru known as the "Shining Path." "Hundreds are flocking to other cities. The hospitals are full. Even the floors are being used, and all medicines are gone. Most of these are Christians. Churches have been bombed with hundreds injured. One church group has lost six pastors and fifty men from one congregation. I know of thirty to fifty families killed trying to leave the area." . . . Several thousand people have been killed, and acts of violence against Christian groups have accelerated in recent months. . . . Evangelization has been banned by the guerrillas.[8]

17

In another recent incident, four Lebanese communist suicide bombers blew up the Voice of Lebanon radio station, which is a conservative Christian radio station in the south of Lebanon. This was a carefully planned attack by the communists who clearly feared the power of the Christian message.

The threat of communism can never be fully understood until one recognizes that it is not just a political philosophy. It is also a religion that not only promises man a utopia, but promises to transform his nature into being a peace-loving creature who loves to work and share. This is one of the reasons why it can capture such total dedication from the underprivileged of the world. (Another reason is that the communists are masters at covering up their record of failure in the Soviet Union and other communist countries where their system has been tried.)

The communists fear a powerful ideal or religion more than they fear military threats. Bible-believing Christians are viewed as one of the most powerful threats of all. They are among the few, for example, who did not break down under the brainwashing tactics used on POWs in the Korean War.

Christianity, which was described by Marx as "the opiate of the people" (meaning, religion anesthetizes the people so that they are willing to continue serving their capitalist masters), has been severely persecuted by the communists in the Soviet Union, Red China, Eastern Europe, North Korea, Cuba, Vietnam, Kampuchea, Laos, Nicaragua, Angola, Zimbabwe, and so on, where millions have been massacred.

Alexander Solzhenitsyn, in giving his acceptance speech for the Templeton Prize on May 10, 1983, best summed up the threat of communism to the Church:

> But the world had never before known a godlessness as organized, militarized, and tenaciously malevolent as that preached by Marxism. Within the philosophical system of Marx and Lenin and at the heart of their psychology, *hatred of God* is the principal driving force, more fundamental than all their political and economic pretensions. [My emphasis.]
>
> Militant atheism is not merely incidental or marginal to communist policy; it is not a side effect, but

the central pivot. To achieve its diabolical ends, communism needs to control a population devoid of religious and national feeling, and this entails a destruction of faith and nationhood.

Communists proclaim both of these objectives openly, and just as openly put them into practice.[9]

I believe that communism will continue to be a great threat to the true Church as it continues to take over more and more countries. History shows that Christians will always be at the top of its hit list.

THE NEED FOR A "COMBAT FAITH"

If we are indeed living in the last days of God's prophetic program of history, which I am convinced we are, then we must expect and prepare for a growing and accelerating persecution of the true Church. I have emphasized "true" Church because the Bible predicts that some of the most severe persecution will come from a false church led by men masquerading as ministers of Christ.

Do not be afraid of these times. As I have so often said, I would rather be alive right now than any other time in history, even if I could have made the choice. We are the generation that is going to see the sudden rending of the clouds and hear the Son of God shout, "Come up here!" Before the sound is fully comprehended we will be in the presence of our Great God and Savior, Jesus the Messiah. Without experiencing death, we will have eternal glorified bodies exactly like His.

But this is not the only reason I'm excited to be alive now. God loves us with an intense and personal care. He will never allow any one of us to be tested above what we are able to stand. Not all of us may experience the coming persecutions, but we all need to learn how to appropriate God's provisions for daily living. Now is the time—before full-fledged persecution begins here—for us to become skilled in combat faith.

Still, if God in His wisdom allows us to go through trials, just listen to what He has provided for each one of us: An experience of perfect inner peace in spite of the adversities, pressures, and problems of life! An experience of joy and inner happiness no matter how difficult and unpleasant our situation! An experience of spiritual stamina and courage, no matter how intense and frightening our circumstances! An experience of unshakable hope and stability when our world and all that is familiar is falling apart! An experience of power when all human strength is gone! An experience of wisdom and confidence, when thrown into an impossible witnessing situation!

You may be saying, "Come on, Hal, that will never be my experience." I don't care how much you may have failed before, how fearful or nervous you may be by nature, how much you are in a habit of worrying about things, how inadequate and inferior you feel about being used of God in these last days: His peace in the midst of your storm can be your constant daily experience!

God delights in taking the least likely candidates and turning them into mighty men and women of faith.

God, Who cannot lie, has promised all of these things to those who will simply claim them by faith. Faith is the key to all these provisions.

What is needed is what I have called "combat faith." With this faith we learn to believe the promises of God in spite of our feelings, emotions, or circumstances. It is a faith that has been trained in the crucible of the trials of life so that it keeps on believing when the going gets tough.

No matter who you are, God says you must learn and develop this kind of faith in order to please Him. I pray, as you examine the Scripture passages that are designed by God to teach us how to learn to believe Him in this way, that God will bless and transform your life experience as He has mine while I was writing about these precious truths.

CHAPTER TWO

The Many Facets of Faith

> Now to the one who works, his wage is not reckoned
> [on the basis of grace], but on the basis of debt. But
> to the one who does not work, but believes in Him
> who justifies the ungodly, his faith is counted as
> righteousness.
>
> Romans 4:4–5 HL

Few subjects in the Bible are more important for us to understand than that of faith. Here are just a few of the things that the Bible declares come through faith: we are born into eternal life through faith; we are declared righteous before God by faith; we are forgiven by faith; we are healed by faith; we understand the mysteries of creation by faith; we learn God's Word by faith; by faith we understand things to come; we walk by faith and not by sight; we overcome the world by faith; we enter God's rest by faith; and we are controlled and impowered by the Holy Spirit by faith. We can only please God by faith, and everything we seek to do for God that is not from the source of faith is sin.

The issue of faith pervades every aspect of our relationship with God and our service for Him. Faith is the source of our strength, our provision, our courage, our guidance, and our victory over the world system, the flesh, and the Devil. Faith is the only thing that can sustain us in the trials and persecutions predicted for the last days.

It is therefore imperative that we understand exactly what faith is, how we get it, and how it grows. For the Christian, no other pursuit is as urgent as the quest for faith. This has always been true, but in the light of the prophetic signs that herald the soon coming of our Lord Jesus, and the inevitable perilous times that precede His coming, it is even more urgent today.

GOD'S DEFINITION OF FAITH

Nowhere in the Bible is a concise definition of faith given. It is described more in terms of what it does, than what it is. God says, **"Now faith is being sure of what we hope for and certain of what we do not see."** (Hebrews 11:1) This definition describes faith in two dimensions, the future, and the present unseen spiritual world. Hope is faith directed toward promised future things, and it gives us certainty in the present that they will be absolutely realized.

The second aspect of true faith enables us to perceive the invisible spiritual world about us, and to operate with confidence in this intangible dimension.

Being Sure of What We Hope For

Abraham beautifully illustrated the first aspect of faith: **"By FAITH Abraham, even though he was past age—and Sarah herself was barren—was ENABLED to become a father BECAUSE HE CONSIDERED HIM FAITHFUL WHO HAD MADE THE PROMISE."** (Hebrews 11:11) Several important facets of faith are brought out in this verse. The object of Abraham's faith was the faithfulness of God. Therefore he was certain that God would keep His promise. This faith-confidence freed God to miraculously enable Abraham to become a father. Faith works because God is faithful and able to keep His promises. The more we learn about God, the more we become certain of the things for which we hope. It is our knowledge of and confidence in the object of faith that grows, not faith itself.

22

Being Certain of What We Do Not See

The second aspect of faith is best illustrated by an incident that happened in the life of Elisha and his disciple Gehazi. The king of Aram, who was trying to invade Israel, was perplexed because the king of Israel knew his every move beforehand. While looking for a traitor among his own officers, he was told that Elisha the prophet was the one who was telling the king of Israel even the secrets that he spoke in his bedroom.

The king of Aram was furious and sent a great army of chariots, cavalry, and infantry by night to surround the city of Dothan where Elisha and his disciple were staying.

Gehazi arose early in the morning, and while he was still wiping sleep from his eyes, he saw that they were completely surrounded by a mighty army of Arameans. In stark terror he ran in to Elisha and exclaimed, **"Oh, my LORD, what shall we do?"** Elisha calmly replied, **"Don't be afraid. Those who are with us are more than those who are with them."**

I'm sure that Gehazi thought, "I always knew there was something strange about this man. Now I know he's nuts! There are over a hundred thousands soldiers out there, and there are only two of us. Why did I ever leave the farm?"

Elisha looked at his disciple and prayed, **"O LORD, OPEN HIS EYES SO HE MAY SEE."** Immediately, the LORD opened Gehazi's eyes so that he could see the invisible. **"Then the LORD opened the servant's eyes, and he looked and saw the hills full of horses and chariots of fire all around Elisha."** (See 2 Kings 6:8-23)

When the LORD opened Gehazi's eyes, he saw an awesome army of angels with horses and chariots of fire standing between them and the enemy army. Elisha was resting in a God-given confidence because by faith he saw the invisible reality of God's promised protection all about him. He demonstrated that **"Faith is being . . . certain of what we do not see."** (Hebrews 11:1)

Science also demonstrates this principle of faith: **"By faith we understand that the worlds were prepared by the word of God, so that what is seen was not made out of things which** are **visible.**" (Hebrews 11:3 NASB) This verse develops how faith enables us to "see" the invisible behind creation. Faith gives us an understanding of the origin of the universe. God spoke it into existence through His omnipotence. Einstein's theory that all tangible matter is made of invisible energy confirms what this inspired writer said nineteen centuries before.

Faith Is Object-Centered

Another important part of the Bible's definition is that in and of itself, faith has no effective power to accomplish God's work. The power in true faith comes from its object. Biblical faith must have an object, and that object is God Himself.

Jesus taught on many occasions about the object of faith. He commanded the following: **"Have faith in God."** (Mark 11:22); and, **"Trust in God; trust also in Me."** (John 14:1) Another teaching of Jesus' bears on this subject: **"The apostles said to the LORD, 'Increase our faith!' He replied, 'If you have faith as small as a mustard seed, you can say to this mulberry tree, "Be uprooted and planted in the sea," and it will obey you.'"** (Luke 17:5–6) The apostles desired the same thing we so often desire, more faith. Jesus' reply is fascinating. The mustard seed is the smallest of seeds. Jesus used that fact to emphasize that it isn't the size of the faith that is important, but rather the power of the One in Whom we place our faith. We need to increase our understanding of God's grace, His love for us, His faithfulness, His awesome power that is available to us. As this grows, even faith as small as a mustard seed is enough to perform stupendous miracles.

Everything about the biblical definition of faith stresses that it is not something *in us* that makes it work, but rather the character of God that makes it work. This prevents faith itself from becoming a human work and gives all the glory of our faith exploits to God.

The Paradox of Faith

In order for mankind to understand how faith works, he must grapple with something that is paradoxical to human experience. The Bible presents faith as the opposite of *human* work. As strange as it may seem, the more *we* work in order to earn God's acceptance, the more hopelessly in debt we become. Jesus sought to shock the religious leaders of His day into that realization when He said to them,

> **I tell you the truth, the tax collectors and the prosti-**
> **tutes are entering the kingdom of God ahead of you.**
> **For John came to you to show you the way of righ-**
> **teousness, and you did not BELIEVE him, but the**
> **tax collectors and the prostitutes did. And even after**
> **you saw this, you did not repent and BELIEVE him.**
> (Matthew 21:31–32)

The way of righteousness is entered by faith, not by the religious works with which these leaders toiled night and day. The prostitutes and tax collectors, who were greedy extortioners, were given God's righteousness in exchange for their faith. When the religionists witnessed their amazing turn to God, and the incredible changes in their lives, they still didn't repent and believe.

Any approach to God by *our* works places us under a merit system. Then we, as fallen creatures, must measure up to God's absolute righteousness, which is an utterly hopeless position. The standard then becomes, **"Whoever keeps the whole law and yet stumbles at just one point is guilty of breaking all of it."** (James 2:10) This is why the Bible teaches that faith is the only way we can relate to God because it assumes no human merit. The moment we attempt to gain *or improve* our relationship with God through *our* good works, we put ourselves under the merit system, and force the Lord to judge us according to the standards of His perfect character which are expressed in the Law of Moses and amplified in the Sermon on the Mount. Many hope that God will judge their religious works in much the same way that some college professors grade their student's exams. But God can't grade on the curve. God must judge us according to the standards of His absolute character. The LORD can not be relative about His righteousness.

Jesus brought this principle out clearly while seeking to

correct the deeply ingrained false interpretations of Judaism that taught that eternal life is earned by keeping the Law of Moses. Jesus was asked by the religious Jews, **" 'What must we do to do the works God requires?' Jesus answered, 'The work of God is this: to believe in the One He has sent.' "** (John 6:28–29) In other words, the only work we can do is not a work at all—it is to believe in the work Jesus accomplished on the cross in our behalf. It is on the basis of this finished work on the cross that the Lord Jesus is free to work in us through the Holy Spirit and produce the righteousness His law requires. All that is required on our part is a moment by moment faith-dependence upon Him.

No Faith, No Fellowship

God had to make it very clear how He views faith because of its indispensable importance to the believer. The most important skill that we must learn as God's children is how to exercise faith, because apart from it we can't have fellowship with God, and without a consistent fellowship with Him, we can't grow to maturity. The following verses illustrate this:

"Whatever is not from faith is sin." (Romans 14:23 NASB) Everything we do that is not done out of the source of faith is sin. This refers not only to the immoral and rebellious things we do, which are obviously sin, but also to the seemingly good things we do for God by our own human ability. The Bible declares that all Christian living and works done apart from faith are unacceptable.

"And without faith it is impossible to please Him." (Hebrews 11:6 NASB) This is an absolute principle for serving God. The LORD never uses someone because he is so good, or because he earned or deserved that privilege.

This is the point, no one is good enough to qualify to be used by God, so faith, which doesn't depend on the merit of the one who is exercising it, is our only means of serving Him.

HOW FAITH RELATES TO GRACE

Faith and grace are mutually dependent. It is impossible to have a strong faith apart from an understanding and appropriation of grace. Grace can only be given to us through faith, and faith can only grow in the sphere of grace. Grace means unmerited favor. If we do anything to try and earn grace, it is no longer unmerited. This is where faith comes in. Faith receives the work of another as a gift. Faith by the very nature of its root meaning implies a cessation of self-effort in order to receive the merit and strength of another. There is no merit earned in receiving a gift by grace through faith.

Faith Is a Gift of God

"For by grace you have been saved through faith; and that not of yourselves, it is the gift of God; not as a result of works, that no one should boast." (Ephesians 2:8–9 NASB) Grace is the means by which we are saved, and faith is the agency through which we receive it as a gift. This verse tells us that even faith itself is a gift of God to us, so we shouldn't become proud of our faith. On this point, God says, **"Do not think of yourself more highly than you ought, but rather think of yourself with sober judgment, in accordance with the measure of faith God has given you."** (Romans 12:3)

"Just as you have once received Christ Jesus the Lord, so keep on walking in Him." (Colossians 2:6 HL) Just as we were once and for all saved "by grace through faith," so we are to walk moment by moment by grace through faith. We continue to live by the same principle with which we were saved.

How Grace Relates to Works

God declared the only acceptable basis upon which His salvation can be given to us: **"Now to the one who works, his wage is not reckoned on the basis of grace, but as what is due. But to the one who does not work, but believes in Him who justifies the ungodly, his faith is reckoned [credited to his account] as righteousness."** (Romans 4:4–5 HL) This passage emphasizes another facet of the meaning of grace. Nothing can be given on the basis of grace to one who feels he has earned it by his own works.

27

Grace and works are mutually exclusive concepts. Where one exists as the basis of gaining acceptance with God the other cannot. Paul argues this very point: **"But if it** [God's salvation] **is by grace, it is no longer on the basis of works, otherwise grace is no longer grace."** (Romans 11:6 NASB)

Good works are important in the life of a believer, but they are the result of a grateful heart that is overflowing with thanksgiving and love for God. Work done with this motive will receive a reward. But works done out of the motive that it will keep you saved will be burned as so much wood, hay, and stubble at the judgment seat of Christ. Such works can only be done out of a motive of fear, guilt, and obligation, all of which are unacceptable to God. The Scripture says, **"For you were called to freedom, brethren; only do not turn your freedom into an opportunity for the flesh, but THROUGH LOVE serve one another."** (Galatians 5:13 NASB)

How Faith Relates to Good Works

How do we reconcile Paul's teaching on faith and works with what James taught?

What good is it, my brothers, if a man claims to have faith but has no deeds? Can such faith save him? . . . You foolish man, do you want evidence that faith without deeds is useless? Was not our ancestor Abraham considered righteous for what he did when he offered his son Isaac on the altar? You see that his faith and his actions were working together, and his faith was made complete by what he did. And the scripture was fulfilled that says, "Abraham believed God, and it was credited to him as righteousness," and he was called God's friend. YOU SEE that a person is justified by what he does and not by faith alone. (James 2:14,20–24)

The simple answer to the seeming conflict between Paul and James is this: true faith always produces good works, but works never produce faith. It all depends on the perspective

from which you start. James emphasizes what man can see—
the works that result from a true faith.

God declared Abraham righteous on the basis of his faith
alone in Genesis 15:6. Over forty years later, Abraham was
willing to offer up his beloved son Isaac as a burnt offering in
response to God's command (See Genesis 22). It took God all
of those forty years to develop such a strong faith in Abraham.
But God declared Abraham righteous on the basis of the faith
He saw in him forty years before, not on the basis of the result
of his faith that had finally matured. The later deed only
proved that the seed of faith Abraham had at the time of salvation was genuine and had grown.

It has been my experience that if you seek to motivate believers with messages of duty, obligation, and guilt, the result
is a lot of "striving in the flesh." But if you emphasize grace,
believers respond with faith and depend upon the Holy Spirit.
As a result, the Holy Spirit produces beautiful deeds through
them. He causes us **"to will and to act according to His
[God's] good purpose."** (Philippians 2:13)

Faith Only Grows in the Atmosphere of Grace

You may be saying, "All right already, Hal. Don't go into
overkill. We got the point." The reason I'm stressing the meaning of grace in relation to faith is because biblical faith is impossible to understand apart from it. True faith gets its very
breath of life from the atmosphere of grace. Just as a fish can't
live and grow very long out of water, so faith can't grow apart
from understanding and operating in the sphere of God's
grace.

FAITH-REST: GOD'S BASE FOR VICTORIOUS LIVING

All of God's miraculous power flows through the believer
who enters into God's supernatural dimension described in
this promise: **"For the one who has entered HIS REST has
himself also rested from his works, as God did from His."**
(Hebrews 4:10 NASB) It is from this dynamic base called

God's rest, which is entered by faith, that all *divinely* approved living must flow.

The *faith-rest* might be called God's twelfth commandment: "Thou shalt not sweat it!" (The eleventh is "Love one another as I have loved you.")

Faith-Rest Operates Through a New World-View

Yet this faith rest is a very difficult concept to communicate because there are simply no parallels in our normal experience. In fact, to enter God's rest our minds have to be reprogrammed with a new world-view and basis of reality. From physical birth our whole life has been lived by a mental attitude called "the human viewpoint." To enter God's rest we must learn to live by "the Divine viewpoint."

Before we go on, let me define these two diametrically opposed viewpoints of life. The human viewpoint (HVP) looks at life through the limitations of human wisdom, strength, and resources.

The Divine viewpoint (DVP), on the other hand, looks at life through God's promise to work in us with His unlimited ability.

I had only been a believer for a short while when I first learned about the principle of the Divine viewpoint. From that time until now it has been one of the most important elements to my understanding of how to live by faith.

Flying By Instruments and the Divine Viewpoint

The following personal experience best illustrated to me the concept of living by the Divine viewpoint. A number of years ago, two dear friends, Johnny Wilkinson (who has since gone to be with the LORD) and Delano Compton, sent their plane to pick me up in Cleveland and bring me to Bluefield, West Virginia. The pilot was a former commander in the Strategic Air Command named Hal Henkle. Everyone affectionately called Hal the "Red Baron" because of his red hair.

The weather was abominable and we were virtually flying on instruments from take-off. Hal, with whom I had already logged many hours in the air, knew that I loved to learn about flying each time I was with him, so he told me to take over the controls. We were still climbing out through extremely heavy clouds and rain when I took over.

I had never tried to fly by instruments alone before, although their function was familiar to me. As we continued climbing, I began to experience some very strange sensations. The turbulence was strong and I got the distinct feeling that we were banking to the left. But the artificial horizon, which shows whether the plane is banking or level, clearly indicated that we were climbing straight and true.

For the first time I could remember, my senses of equilibrium and feel were deceiving me. I felt as if we were going down, and kept fighting the urge to pull back on the controls. Then there was a feeling as if we were banking again, only this time to the right. Each time, my senses and the instruments were in conflict. It took all my strength of will and concentration to keep from reacting to the false signals my physical senses were giving me. I realized that believing the flight instruments *in spite of my feelings* meant life or death.

During the flight, I recalled a sobering taped conversation between an air controller and a pilot who was in severe trouble. He was too low on fuel to fly to an airport that wasn't socked in by the weather and he had never flown by instruments before. The pilot had no choice but to let the plane down into the heavy overcast and seek to land. The air controller sought to help him as much as possible. He cleared the area of other aircraft and vectored the pilot for a straight-in approach to the airport.

The pilot's voice sounded confident as he descended into the clouds. Yet within a few minutes he was screaming that his aircraft was out of control. The air controller kept telling him that if he would let go of the controls, the plane, which was now upside down, would right itself. The pilot, who had had many hours' experience at visual flying, could not stop following his feelings instead of believing his instruments. Minutes later he was killed as his plane crashed, completely out of control. His very skill at visual flying confused him. His sharply trained senses felt the plane's movements and kept overriding his confidence in the instruments.

It is often said that a pilot "flies by the seat of his pants." There's a lot of truth to that, because a pilot learns to respond to the pressure exerted by gravity on his seat as the plane banks, climbs, or dives. The balance mechanism in the inner ear also causes him to anticipate and correct movements. But these feelings can be completely deceived and confused without the natural horizon as a reference point.

I thanked God that the "Red Baron" was sitting next to me and could bail me out if I got in trouble. We made it to Bluefield, flying in the clouds most of the way. I experienced many more recurrences of the strange sensation of the battle between my feelings and the instruments. I thought, "How similar this whole experience is to living by the Divine viewpoint of life through faith."

Some Close Parallels

There are some close parallels between flying by instruments and living by the kind of faith the Bible describes. The Bible contains our flight and communication instruments, the LORD Jesus is our air controller, and the Holy Spirit is our co-pilot.

In coping with the daily challenges of life, we are tempted to follow our emotions, feelings, and human reason instead of the Word of God. We are so accustomed to trusting our feelings and emotions that it is very hard to change the habit. Our entire framework of reality has been formed on the basis of the human viewpoint.

As we learn and believe the Scriptures, the attitudes of our minds are reprogrammed to the Divine viewpoint. Then, as stated before, the Divine viewpoint begins to look at life, not from the standpoint of natural abilities and talents, but through God's unlimited power.

Most Christians are trying to live the Christian life "flying by the seat of their pants." This will seem to work satisfactorily until we enter some of the storms and heavy overcast conditions of life. Then the very self-confidence we have developed through our human abilities will hinder trusting God's instrument.

But when we are born spiritually into the family of God, we receive a new nature that enables us to perceive and function in the spiritual realm. This new nature has a new means of perception, a sixth sense called faith. Walking by faith is a skill that has to be learned, just as the pilot has to learn how to fly "blind," trusting only his instruments. We have to learn to **"walk by faith and not by sight"** (2 Corinthians 5:7 HL), trusting only in God's promises.

Our spiritual nature has to grow and learn to function in the atmosphere of the Divine viewpoint. This new world of spiritual reality can only be found in God's Word.

If you as a Christian seek to cope with life through the HVP, and go by your feelings instead of by what God says, your life will crash as surely as did the pilot who couldn't let go of his feelings and trust the airplane's instruments.

But on the other hand, if you learn to fly through the storms of life by God's instruments, His promises, you will crack the faith barrier and soar into that most incredible of all human experiences, God's rest, and be brought safely home.

Only God fully knows the impact that all these faith-truths from the Word of God had upon my badly damaged soul. They not only changed my life, but helped save my sanity as well. Through these truths, God produced in me an undefeatable confidence. Only it wasn't self-confidence, it was **Christ**-confidence. God developed in me the kind of confidence that Paul expressed: **"I can do all things through Christ who keeps on strengthening me."** (Philippians 4:13 HL)

It was this faith-produced **Christ**-confidence that enabled me, a college dropout who barely finished high school, to complete successfully a four-year Masters of Theology course with a major in New Testament Greek; and later to be declared the bestselling nonfiction author of the seventies by the *New York Times,* even though I had never been trained as a writer. I bear witness that only God could have produced such works in me, and I rejoice in giving the glory to Him.

The Faith-Rest Defined

The faith-rest, briefly described, is that principle taught in the Word of God by which we enter a divinely provided dynamic rest from struggling to live for God. This is done by believing the promises of God's Word, which releases God to work in and through us with His mighty power and wisdom. Even the indispensable means of living the Christian life called "walking in the Spirit" is appropriated by believing God's promises of the Holy Spirit's ministry to us.

As I learned all these various principles of faith, I began to understand that God delighted in taking that which the world considered useless and making it into something that would demonstrate His grace and power to change human nature.

This book is about these truths, which are the very source of our spiritual life. Because of the proven effectiveness of these truths, I share them with a great deal of joy and anticipation.

CHAPTER THREE

Cracking the "Faith Barrier"

> There remains, then, a Sabbath-rest for the people
> of God; for anyone who enters God's rest also rests
> from his own work, JUST AS GOD did from His.
> Let us, therefore, make every effort to enter that
> rest . . .
>
> Hebrews 4:9–11a

I was fascinated to watch the movie *The Right Stuff* and to remember those exciting days when daring young men risked their lives to crack through that seemingly impenetrable barrier posed by the speed of sound. As pilots approached that speed, great turbulence built up against the airplane. The air literally couldn't get out of the way fast enough, and piled up in front of the leading edges of the aircraft, causing violent buffeting. This also caused aerodynamic changes in the airflow over the control surfaces, which in turn made the craft almost impossible to control. The controls would freeze and become inoperable, and sometimes their functions would even reverse. Many brave men died in the conquest of what became known as "the sound barrier."

Then one day, a World War II ace named Chuck Yeager climbed into the cockpit of a little experimental rocket-powered aircraft dubbed the Bell X-1, which was slung under the belly of a B-29 bomber. High up in the stratosphere he dropped clear. He was thrown back against the seat as he ignited the rocket engines and rapidly accelerated toward what the test pilots had nicknamed the "demon that lurks at the speed of sound."

As Yeager accelerated, approaching the speed of sound, the plane began to shake violently. It seemed that it would disintegrate at any second. The control stick shook so violently that Chuck, who concealed that he had broken several ribs the night before and had little use of his right arm, could hardly hold on to it. Just as it seemed the airplane was breaking up, there was a loud boom and all became quiet and serene inside the cockpit. The buffeting stopped, the controls responded again, and the Mach meter had gone off the scale. Man had at last cracked the sound barrier. There were still great pressures on the outside of the little craft, but the turbulent air had shifted from the front to back. He was flying smooth and stable, and the screaming noise and violent air was left behind as he bolted toward the dark blue of the edge of earth's atmosphere. Yeager had unwittingly launched man on the first giant step toward the conquest of space.

Some thirty years ago I heard my pastor use this phenomenon to illustrate a tremendous spiritual principle that I've never forgotten. There are some amazing parallels between cracking the sound barrier and cracking the "faith barrier."

Each believer has to crack the faith barrier, which is also very difficult to penetrate. Though it takes a great deal of speed to crack the sound barrier, to crack the faith barrier we must *stand still and exert no human effort*. When we approach the faith barrier, there are great pressures and turbulences that have built up in our lives from seeking to cope with our problems in our own strength. The resistance comes from our trying to cope by the same old means of the flesh we have used all our lives. It's very difficult to let go and simply believe the LORD. But when we crack through the faith barrier by believing God's promises, we then enter into that most wonderful of Christian experiences called "God's rest." The pressures and problems may still exist, but there is a peace inside our hearts. Incredible works are produced through us while we are resting in the LORD, because it is not our efforts that are their source, but the Holy Spirit's.

Cracking the faith barrier illustrates the most essential

technique that we must practice each day. It is basic to living a victorious and fruitful life for the LORD.

The most important book that introduces the principle of how to crack the faith barrier and enter God's rest is the Epistle to the Hebrews. The LORD inspired the writer to pull together many great examples of this God-given rest from the Old Testament. We can only enter this rest by faith.

In order to understand the exhortations concerning faith, it is important to know a little of the background of the book of Hebrews.

The letter was written to the Hebrew-Christian community that lived in and about Jerusalem. It was written around A.D. 66 or 67, just before the siege of Jerusalem by the Roman Tenth legion which began in A.D. 68. Jerusalem and the Temple were destroyed by them in A.D. 70.

There was a severe persecution of Christians during the few years before the siege. This is referred to in chapter ten, verses thirty-two through thirty-nine. The Roman governor was confiscating all Christian property and giving 10 percent of it to the informant who turned them in (usually a zealot of Judaism). The exposed Christian and his whole family were then dragged off to prison through streets filled with jeering and mocking crowds (see Hebrews 10:32-34).

Hebrew Christians were exposed most commonly through the test of whether they offered an animal sacrifice in the Temple during the feast season. This could easily be checked by the priests, since all Jews did this at least once a year. In order to escape persecution, some Christians began to minimize the distinctions between Judaism and the New Covenant, which Jesus the Messiah had established by His blood, and returned to offering animal sacrifices.

God spoke against this compromise with one of the most severe warnings in all the Bible. He called it **"crucifying the Son of God all over again and subjecting Him to public disgrace."** (Hebrews 6:6) The reason is clear. The animal sacrifices prescribed under the law of Moses were [types] and graphic previews of the Messiah's sacrificial death for sin. Jesus the Messiah's substitutionary death on the cross once and for all fulfilled what these continually offered sacrifices only foreshadowed. He is **"the lamb of God, who TOOK AWAY the**

sins of the world." (John 1:29 HL) Animal sacrifices only temporarily covered man's sin out of God's sight; Jesus removed sin as a barrier between man and God forever through a once-and-for-all sacrifice (see Hebrews 10:1–14).

For the believers to offer animal sacrifices after coming to the knowledge of this truth was tantamount to **"treading under foot the Son of God, counting as unclean the blood of the covenant by which he was sanctified, and insulting the Spirit of Grace."** (Hebrews 10:29 HL) It was in effect saying that the Messiah's sacrifice wasn't sufficient to save them from sin.

This great sin was keeping them out of fellowship with the LORD and making it impossible to grow into maturity. In fact they had retrogressed in spiritual maturity to the point where **"they needed to be taught the elementary truths of God's word all over again, and needed milk instead of solid food."** (Hebrews 5:11–14 HL)

The LORD deals with this situation by giving both the sternest warnings, and the greatest instruction and encouragement on how to enter His rest by faith in the face of severe trials and frightening times. The LORD proceeds to give the grandest explanation of how to walk by faith in His promises in the midst of intense trials.

I believe that the temptation to compromise our confession of faith in Christ will soon be much greater than **anything yet known** in the Western world. This is why I believe that the message the LORD gave to the Hebrew believers concerning the faith-rest during their period of persecution is one of the major biblical passages relevant to the Church's preparation for its last days.

INTRODUCTION TO GOD'S REST

The Holy Spirit introduces us to that experience available to every believer called **"God's rest."** I am going to quote the entire biblical context, which I urge you to read carefully. Note particularly how many times **"rest"** is mentioned. Note also the serious consequences that fell upon the generation of Israelites who failed to enter that **"rest"** during the Exodus out of Egypt, and why they failed to enter the **"rest."**

(To help emphasize the most important points, I am putting some words in all capital letters and making certain notes within the text.) The writer to the Hebrews said:

Therefore, just as the Holy Spirit says,
"Today if you hear His voice,
Do not harden your hearts as when they provoked
     Me,
As in the day of trial in the wilderness,
Where your fathers tried Me by TESTING Me,
And saw My works for FORTY YEARS.
"Therefore I was angry with this generation,
And said, 'They always go astray in their heart;
And they DID NOT KNOW MY WAYS'; As I
     swore in My wrath,
'They shall not enter MY REST.'" (Quoted in
     Hebrews from Psalm 95:7–11)

Take care, brethren, lest there should be in any one of you AN EVIL, UNBELIEVING HEART, in falling away from the living God. But encourage one another day after day, as long as it is still called "Today," lest any one of you be hardened by the deceitfulness of sin. For we have become partakers of [partners with] Christ, if we hold fast the beginning of our assurance firm until the end; while it is said, "TODAY if you hear His voice,/Do not harden your hearts, as when they provoked Me."

For who provoked Him when they had heard? Indeed, did not all those who came out of Egypt led by Moses? [Answer: all except Moses, Aaron, Caleb, and Joshua] And with whom was He angry for forty years? Was it not with those who sinned, whose bodies fell in the wilderness? And to whom did He swear that they should not enter HIS REST, but to those who were disobedient? And so we see that they were not able to enter because of UNBELIEF.

Therefore, let us fear lest, while a PROMISE remains of entering HIS REST, any one of you should seem to have come short of IT [namely, fail to enter

His rest by persistently not believing the promises]. For indeed we have had good news preached to us, just as they also; but the word they heard did not profit them, because it was not united by FAITH in those who heard. For WE WHO HAVE BELIEVED ENTER THAT REST, just as He has said, "As I swore in My wrath,/They shall not enter MY REST," although His works were finished from the foundation of the world. For He has thus said somewhere concerning the seventh day, "And God rested on the seventh day from all His works"; and again in this passage, "They shall not enter MY REST."

Since therefore it remains for some to enter IT, and those who formerly had good news preached to them failed to enter because of disobedience, He again fixes a certain day, "Today," saying through David after so long a time [David wrote Psalm 95, which is quoted here, about four hundred years after the Exodus] just as has been said before, "Today if you hear His voice,/Do not harden your hearts." For if Joshua had given them REST, He would not have spoken of another day after that.

There remains therefore a SABBATH REST for the people of God. For the one who has entered HIS REST has himself also RESTED from his works, as God did from His.

Let us therefore be diligent to enter that REST, lest anyone fall through following the same example of disobedience. (Hebrews 3:7–4:11 NASB)

As you read through the above passage, I'm sure you gathered that the main point of its message is that we *must* enter God's rest, and that there is a certain urgency in not putting off the decision to do so.

You should have also noted that the only way to enter God's rest is by believing His promises. Two things in this passage were revolutionary to my Christian life when I learned them.

First, the inspired writer carefully establishes that God has **"His rest"** available for each generation. He did this by showing that David wrote about the rest that was promised to the Exodus generation being available to his generation, even though it was about four hundred years later. In this passage, the Holy Spirit gives us a masterful demonstration of comparing Scripture with Scripture in order to establish an irrefutable case. Through this, the Holy Spirit proved from the Old Testament Scriptures that **"God's rest"** was available to me today.

Second, this passage clearly establishes the precedent that the biblical promises made to other people at other times are still available and valid to us. We can claim all of these promises as long as the circumstances and conditions are similar.

In fact, verse one of chapter four commands us to fear establishing a pattern of *failing* to claim God's promises. This caused me to realize that the more than seven thousand promises in the Bible are mine to claim. I will not need these promises in heaven. They are only useful for my needs in this life. I will have no needs in eternity.

After I discovered this truth as a young believer, the Old Testament immediately became alive to me. I learned the truth of what Paul meant when he said, **"For whatever was written in earlier times was written for our instruction, that through the perseverance and the encouragement of [produced by] the Scriptures we might have hope."** (Romans 15:4 NASB)

I memorized hundreds of Bible promises, and started to categorize them in a notebook. That was one of the most important things I ever did. These promises have saved me so many times in so many ways. And more than once they literally saved my life. It is for this reason that I believe that the meaning of God's rest, and just how to enter it, are among the most important truths for a believer to learn.

THE MEANING OF GOD'S REST

What is the exact meaning of God's rest in Hebrews chapters three and four? Some interpreters have said that it is an illustration of entering salvation through faith in Christ, but in the typology of the passage, entering the promised land of Canaan is a picture of God's people entering His rest and con-

41

quering through faith. If entering the promised land and God's rest were a picture of entering salvation, then even Moses and Aaron were not saved, because they were not allowed the enter the land. Of all that generation, only Joshua and Caleb were allowed to enter the promised land.

The Passover and Red sea deliverance were the Divine types to portray salvation. When Israel entered the promised land, they took possession of it by means of war. Though they ran after the enemy with drawn sword, inside themselves they were resting by faith in the promises of God.

This is the picture that God draws to illustrate His rest and how to live the Christian life today. Though we are in the midst of a *great spiritual war,* we can rest inwardly and have perfect peace. The Holy Spirit clothes Himself with the one who believes God's promises, and then works through him. The LORD promised through Paul, **"The requirements of the Law are fulfilled IN us** [not by us], **who do not walk according to the flesh** [human ability], **but according to the Spirit,"** and, **"For it is God who is working in you to will and to act according to His good purpose."** (Romans 8:4 and Philippians 2:13 HL)

Our New Sabbath

The rest is further illustrated and defined by a quotation concerning God's rest on the seventh day of creation. Have you ever asked yourself why God rested? Do you think He rested because He was tired? Of course not! God rested because all the work for providing mankind's every need was finished in six days.

We are invited to enter God's Sabbath rest on a moment by moment continuing basis. We can cease from our own human labors even as God ceased from His Divine work of creation. This is why there is no outward Sabbath day of rest commanded for the Christian. Instead, we are to have a continual Sabbath rest every day in our souls.

We can rest because God has provided everything necessary for us to live a full, victorious life, filled with inner peace, purpose, Divine direction, power for service, confidence, and inner joy. All of this is realized no matter how great the outer pressure, no matter how great the adversity, no matter how perplexing the problems, if we learn and believe the promises of His Word.

If we continually fail to believe God's promises, and instead, *worry* and *complain* about life's circumstances, we are in danger of developing a pattern of unbelief that the LORD says is an **"evil unbelieving heart that causes us to fall away from the living God."** (Hebrews 3:12b HL) This is not a description of the many other terrible sins the Exodus generation committed, but of the sin God considered the worst of all—failure to believe His promises. This was the root sin that caused all the other sins. Even though we are still God's children and bound for heaven, a lack of faith will ensure us the same miserable existence in this life that the Israelites had during forty years of discipline in the Sinai desert.

GOD'S FAITH COURSE NO. 101

The LORD has illustrated for all generations the principles and the dynamics of belief and unbelief through the history of His dealings with Israel. Israel is a picture of the believer's soul. God deals with us as individuals by the same principles He dealt with Israel, or perhaps corporately—with the nation of Israel as a whole.

The LORD sets up a clear typological model for our course in "Faith 101" through Israel's Exodus experience:

Israel in Egypt is a picture of unsaved humanity laboring in slavery to sin and Satan (typified by Pharaoh);

Israel's keeping of the Passover is a Divinely ordained passion play to illustrate salvation through the substitutionary sacrifice of God's greater lamb—Jesus the Messiah;

Israel's deliverance at the Red sea is a picture of redemption, by God's power, from the slave market of sin and the authority of Satan the slave-master;

Israel's initial time in the Sinai portrays spiritual immaturity; Israel's return and continuance in the Sinai is a picture of the barren and unfulfilled life of a believer walking in unbelief and carnality; (There's nothing wrong with being a "spiritual baby" if you are a new believer, but if you continue to be one, you're in big trouble).

Israel possessing the promised land demonstrates the victorious life of a Spirit-empowered believer who has cracked the faith barrier—entered God's rest by faith in God's promises.

The principles of victory through cracking the faith barrier and entering God's rest are fully demonstrated through the lives of the Old Testament characters. The historical background for the message we have surveyed in Hebrews covers the period from the Exodus of the Israelites out of Egypt under Moses to the possession of the promised land under Joshua.

This great historical drama actually begins with a parent's faith—in this case, that of Moses' mother. She passed on to Moses the "baton of faith" so that he could run in life's greatest relay race whose goal is the eternal purpose of God. This inherited faith prepared Moses for one of the greatest decisions of all times, a decision that actually altered the course of world history. But first, let's examine an earlier example of a parent's faith. . . .

CHAPTER FOUR

The Impact of Parents' Faith

I will utter things hidden from of old—things we
have heard and known, things our fathers have told
us. We will not hide them from our children; we will
tell the next generation the praiseworthy deeds of
the LORD, His power, and the wonders He has done.

Psalm 78:2–4 HL

THE HERITAGE OF FAITH

One of the most important ways that faith is passed on is
through parents teaching their children about the wonderful
trustworthiness and faithfulness of God. Since true faith is object centered, we must know about the character and deeds of
the One in Whom we place our trust. The LORD commands
parents to diligently teach their children about how He delivered the helpless who believed in Him through mighty wonders and deeds of power.

Down through the history of human endeavor, mankind
has honored his greatest exploits with various sorts of "halls of
fame." God also has a hall of fame for His heroes of faith, and
He gives us a sampling of it in Hebrews chapter eleven. Every
person named in this chapter achieved what is in God's estimation an extraordinary performance of faith. Their examples
of faith form a rich background from which the Holy Spirit
teaches us about how to believe God in every sort of situation.

There are a number of very special parents God commends in His hall of fame. Each one of those commended not only had faith, but also passed it on to his children. One of those parents was Abraham.

Abraham's Greatest Sacrifice

The LORD gave many incredible promises to Abraham. God told him that he would have a son, and that through him He would make a great nation; that he would bless the world through a seed that would descend from him; and that he would inherit the land of Canaan as an everlasting inheritance.

It was apparent to Abraham that everything promised to him depended upon the LORD giving him a son. But he was concerned since he was already seventy-five years old, and his wife was sixty-five years old and barren.

Abraham sought to believe the LORD's promise for the next eleven years. But when God delayed fulfilling it, he decided to take matters into his own hands. Abraham, at his wife Sarah's suggestion, took her handmaiden Hagar, and slept with her. Ishmael was born as a result of that attempt to fulfill God's promise by human means. Israel is still suffering today because of that little lapse of faith, because Ishmael became the principal father of the Arab nations. The Arab–Israeli conflict started in the tents of Abraham and has continued for four thousand years.

The LORD waited thirteen more years after that escapade before He appeared to Abraham again. God told the ninety-nine-year-old Abraham that the following year, his wife would have a son. Abraham laughed out of joy at this announcement. He had finally learned after leaning on everything else except God that he could trust the LORD to fulfill every one of His promises, even if they were humanly impossible.

However, Sarah, who was listening in from behind a partition, laughed to herself and said,

"After I am worn out and my master is old, will I now have this pleasure?" Then the LORD said to Abraham, "Why did Sarah laugh and say, 'Will I

**really have a child, now that I am old?' IS ANY-
THING TOO HARD FOR THE LORD? . . ."** Sarah
**was afraid, so she lied and said, "I did not laugh."
But He said, "Yes, you did laugh."** (Genesis 18:12–
15)

Imagine trying to lie to the LORD who knows our every
thought!

The LORD showed His sense of humor again when He
commanded them to name the boy Isaac, which means
"laughter." Every time they said the boy's name, Sarah was
reminded that she had laughed in unbelief when God foretold
his birth.

Isaac grew to manhood, and Abraham trained him in the
lessons of faith. He taught Isaac all about the mighty deeds the
LORD had done, and about all the promises God had sworn
by an oath to fulfill to him and his descendants.

All of Abraham's love and dreams were wrapped up in
his boy. Isaac was his father's heart. Yet when Isaac grew to his
late twenties, God suddenly spoke to Abraham and told him
to take his only son and to offer him as a burnt sacrifice to
Him. Can you imagine the emotions that must have gripped
Abraham's heart? How could God tell him to take the one he
loved above all other things, the one through whom God Himself had promised certain unconditional blessings, and put
him to death?

In spite of his inner turmoil and all the seeming contradic-
tions, Abraham in obedient faith set off with his beloved son
for a three-day journey to a special mountain to which God
directed them.

Abraham demonstrated an almost incredible faith when
he arrived at the mountain for the sacrifice and said to his servants, **"Stay here with the donkey while I and the boy go over
there. *WE* will worship and then *WE* will come back to you."**
(Genesis 22:5) Did you get that? Abraham said, **"*WE* will come
back to you."** Abraham had put together all the facts: God had
promised the boy to him and by a miracle had fulfilled the
promise; all of God's promised blessings depended upon
Isaac living and having children of his own; so if God required
him to offer Isaac as a sacrifice, He would have to raise him up

from the dead immediately, or else His Word would be invalidated—which Abraham knew could not happen. I don't know about you, but that's such a wonderful example of faith it gives me goose bumps.

Isaac demonstrated that he also had great faith by willingly obeying his father and climbing up upon the altar and submitting to being bound on the pile of wood as a burnt offering. Isaac was young and strong and could have easily resisted, but he was willing to believe God and trust his father even unto death.

Just as Abraham was about to sacrifice his son, God stopped him. The LORD called out to him and said, **"Abraham! Abraham! . . . Do not lay a hand on the boy. . . . Do not do anything to him. Now I know that you fear** [reverently trust] **God, because you have not withheld from me your son, your only son."** (Genesis 22:11–12) God had put Abraham to the ultimate test of faith and found him trustworthy.

Because of Abraham's faith, we gentiles as well as the Israelites have been blessed right up to this present hour, for God said to him, **"I swear by myself, declares the LORD, that because you have done this and have not withheld your son, your only son, I will surely bless you and make your descendants as numerous as the stars in the sky and as the sand on the seashore. . . . and through your offspring** [seed, namely, the Messiah] **all nations** [gentiles] **on earth will be blessed, because you have obeyed Me."** (Genesis 22:15–18) As a gentile, I am very grateful to Abraham.

God provided a ram as a substitutionary sacrifice in place of Isaac. Abraham named that particular spot on Mount Moriah **Jehovah Jireh,** which means "The LORD will Provide." Two thousand years later on that exact spot, the LORD did provide. In God's case, however, He could not spare His own son, but offered him up as an atoning sacrifice for the sins of a rebellious world. Abraham's experience illustrated for us something of how the father-heart of God must have felt when Jesus was brutally executed upon a cross.

In this great test, Abraham passed on the heritage of faith to his son—and to us.

God's Commendation of Moses' Parents

Moses' parents were also commended in God's hall of fame: **"By faith Moses' parents hid him for three months after he was born, because they saw he was no ordinary child, and they were not afraid of the king's edict."** (Hebrews 11:23)

The historical context in which this courageous faith occurred was this: a Pharaoh came to power who was unfamiliar with Joseph, a Hebrew slave who by the providence of God had risen to be a vice-regent in Egypt some three centuries earlier.

The new king did not take note of the fact that Joseph's family had been brought to Egypt by order of a previous Pharaoh in appreciation of Joseph's faithful service, which, among other things, had saved Egypt from a terrible famine.

This new Pharaoh saw the Hebrews only as a potential threat to his kingdom, because after nearly 320 years in Egypt, their population had exploded. They were a physically hardy race, composed mostly of shepherds and farmers. Pharaoh feared that in time of war they would join with Egypt's enemies and overthrow his kingdom.

Pharaoh sought to kill off some of their numbers by forcing them to build his cities under ruthless slave masters and inhuman conditions. But the more ruthlessly they were treated, the more they multiplied.

In desperation, Pharaoh ordered all Hebrew midwives to kill every male child at birth. But they secretly refused to carry out the order, saying that the strong Hebrew women were giving birth before they arrived. When Pharaoh couldn't stealthily kill the Hebrew males, he openly ordered them thrown into the river to drown. (From Exodus, chapter one.)

In this terrible perilous time, a married couple from the tribe of Levi gave birth to a son. The Scripture says, **"When she** [Moses' mother] **saw that he was a fine** [literally, **"extraordinary, beautiful"**] **child, she hid him for three months."** (Exodus 2:2) Moses' mother saw something extraordinary about the child that she perceived made him special to God. This is the interpretation given us by the Holy Spirit through Stephen's (the Church's first martyr) great message, **"At that** time Moses was born, and he was no ordinary child." (Acts 7:20)

So, by faith, she disobeyed the king's order. If caught, she, the boy, and his father would be put to death.

When Moses' mother hid the baby as long as she possibly could, she did something that took even more faith. She made a little boat of papyrus reeds and waterproofed it with tar and pitch. Then, having done all she could to save the baby's life, she, by faith, trusted the baby into God's hand. She put her baby into the little boat, covered it with a lid, and left it among the reeds on the bank of a river. She had put her child on God's altar and trusted Him to do something to save the baby's life.

It is obvious that Moses' mother expected God to save her baby, because she left him at just the time and place where Pharaoh's daughter usually took her daily bath. The Egyptians, especially the royalty, bathed every morning in the Nile as part of their religious ritual.

Miriam, Moses' sister, stood at a distance to see what God would do.

Then Pharaoh's daughter went down to the Nile to bathe, and her attendants were walking along the river bank [probably to check for crocodiles]. She saw the basket among the reeds and sent her slave girl to get it. She opened it and saw the baby. He was crying, and she felt sorry for him. "This is one of the Hebrew babies," she said.

Then his sister asked Pharaoh's daughter, "Shall I go and get one of the Hebrew women to nurse the baby for you?"

"Yes, go," she answered. And the girl went and got the baby's mother. Pharaoh's daughter said to her, "Take this baby and nurse him for me, and I will pay you." So the woman took the baby and nursed him. When the child grew older, she took him to Pharaoh's daughter and he became her son. She named him MOSES, saying, "I drew him out of the water" [The name Moses means "to draw out"]. (Exodus 2:5–10)

Talk about God answering faith! I never study this incident without being overwhelmed by the grace and faithfulness of the LORD. Just look at what the LORD did for this desperate mother, who, in spite of the impossible circumstances, trusted God to do something extraordinary to save her baby's life:

First, the LORD did save the baby's life.

Second, the LORD not only gave the baby boy back to his mother, but, also arranged for royal protection as well.

Third, she was paid wages to nurse her own child!

Fourth, she was allowed to keep baby Moses until he was about six years old, the normal time of weaning in those days. It was during that time that she apparently was able to indelibly sow in his heart the knowledge of Israel's God and the hope resulting from His promises to the Israelis. Later in life, Moses knew enough about the hope of Israel, and the promised Messiah, to turn down the throne of Egypt in order to follow Him. Since he was raised in the courts of Pharaoh, and apparently had no further contact with his mother or his people, he must have received his basic spiritual training during his earliest childhood.

Fifth, in the gracious providence of God, Moses was officially adopted as Pharaoh's daughter's son and became the heir apparent to the throne of Egypt. As a result, he was trained in all the knowledge of the Egyptians, which at that time was the most advanced in the world.

Can't you imagine this Jewish mother following the career of her son from afar and telling her friends, with understandable pride, "Look at my son the prince!"

This dear courageous mother's faith was passed on to her son, who became Israel's long awaited deliverer, and one of the greatest men in history. This mother had cracked the faith barrier when she defied the king's order and later committed her baby to the LORD on the banks of the Nile. She was sure of her future hope, and certain of the invisible God's providential care.

Her example teaches us that we can never lose when we trust the LORD, especially with our children.

ENCOURAGEMENT FOR TODAY'S PARENTS

In today's world, there is no way for parents to raise and train children successfully in the ways of the LORD, without cracking the faith barrier, just as Moses' parents did. We must learn and believe the promises and admonitions of God's Word in this all-important responsibility.

Vast technological changes in travel and communication have had a tremendous impact on the kind of cultural environment we live in today. In previous centuries, the level of immorality and evil accepted in one city or country usually took years to spread to rural areas and other countries. It used to take years for the level of immorality accepted in, say, New York City to work its way into acceptability in Iowa. But this is not the case today. A new low of morality in, for instance, London becomes the "in thing" in Fresno, California, virtually overnight. Television, rock music, movies, magazines all have a profound and instant worldwide effect on the life-styles and thinking of our youth in particular. This fits in exactly with what Jesus prophesied concerning the last days.

Our children face an environment where the Bible and all absolute truth are rejected, particularly by the media, the movie industry, and the secular educational system. Free sex, pornography, rampant drug and alcohol abuse, dishonesty, stealing, and so on are often considered acceptable.

To bring up your child to follow the LORD in a generation so diametrically opposed to godliness requires faith. It also requires prayer, Holy Spirit–produced love, grace, and wisdom, commitment and discipline (on your part), and a determination to teach him or her the Word of God. Let me share some of the counsel the Bible gives to us parents.

Concerning Teaching Children

These words, which I am commanding you today, shall be on your heart; and you shall teach them diligently to your sons and shall talk of them when you sit in your house and when you walk by the way and

when you lie down and when you rise up. (Deuteronomy 6:6–7 NASB)

> **For He established a testimony in Jacob,**
> **And appointed a law in Israel,**
> **Which He commanded our fathers,**
> **That they should TEACH them to their**
> **children,**
> **That the generation to come might**
> **know, even the children yet to be**
> **born,**
> **That they may arise and tell them to**
> **their children,**
> **That they SHOULD PUT THEIR**
> **CONFIDENCE IN GOD,**
> **And not FORGET THE WORKS of**
> **God,**
> **But keep His commandments,**
> **And not be like their fathers,**
> **A stubborn and rebellious generation,**
> **A generation that did not prepare its**
> **heart,**
> **And whose spirit was not faithful to**
> **God.** (Psalms 78:5–8 NASB)

The great importance of teaching the children the Word of God is constantly repeated throughout the Old Testament. Children cannot trust a God that they do not know. We are commanded to recount to our children the mighty acts of God performed in history, and the factors of faith the people demonstrated that caused Him to do them.

Some of the most important lessons of faith we can pass on to our children are the ones we've experienced personally. I have found that it is very helpful to keep a journal of answered prayers and situations where the LORD answered our faith. Children never tire of hearing about the mighty acts of God in their own family's history. In this way, they are able to personally experience what you teach concerning God's faithfulness.

Incredible feats of faith can be traced directly to parents teaching their children about the character of God and His ways. David, who became the greatest king in the history of Israel, by faith killed a giant when he was a young teenage boy, and by that feat rallied the defeated army of Israel to victory. He obviously had learned at a very early age through the exploits of his ancestor, Caleb, that God was in the giant-killing business. He had also been taught about God's faithfulness and purpose for Israel, and on that basis believed God for miracles.

This same characteristic was certainly evident in the life of Moses. His parents prepared him even as an infant by teaching him about the God of Israel, as we will see in the next chapter.

In Israel's own history, we can also see that when God's Word stopped being the focus of the family and was no longer taught to the children, apostasy and destruction were the consequences.

The New Testament doesn't add much to the child-raising instructions of the Old, but rather draws upon them: **"Children, obey your parents in the LORD, for this is right. 'Honor your father and mother'—which is the first commandment with a promise—'that it may go well with you and that you may enjoy long life on the earth.'"** (Ephesians 6:1–3)

Still, one very important instruction to the parent *is* added in the New Testament: **"Fathers, do not exasperate your children; instead, bring them up in the training and instruction of the LORD."** (Ephesians 6:4) This emphasizes that all the training of our children must be done with Spirit-produced love and grace. Discipline must not be administered in anger, but with the calm firmness and consistency that the Holy Spirit promises to give us.

Moses' parents left us a wonderful example of faith to follow!

CHAPTER FIVE

An Act of Faith That Changed History

He is no fool who gives up what he cannot keep to gain what he cannot lose.

Jim Elliott (martyred in the Amazon)

Moses is cited in God's hall of fame for many exploits of faith. The account of his life in Egypt, the decision he made to leave, and the events that caused him to return to Egypt form rich and imperative lessons of faith needed to understand and appropriate the teachings of the Epistle to the Hebrews on entering God's rest.

In Stephen the martyr's message to the Sanhedrin, he said of Moses, **"When he was placed outside [by the Nile], Pharaoh's daughter took him and brought him up as her own son. Moses was educated in all the wisdom of the Egyptians and was powerful in speech and action."** (Acts 7:21–22)

In God's providence, Moses received an extraordinary training. There are some good extra-biblical sources telling of Moses' early life (such as *The Antiquities* by Josephus) that help amplify the scriptural account. As mentioned before, Moses was educated in *all* the wisdom of the Egyptians. This meant that he was trained in the leading educational center of the world of that time. He learned engineering, advanced mathematics, physics, astronomy, military science, history, several languages, and more.

We still marvel today at some of the feats of engineering, mathematics, and astronomy that were accomplished in that era. Egyptian culture had become highly developed during this period. Egypt was the envy of the civilized world.

When Stephen said that Moses **"was powerful in speech and action,"** he was referring to the exceptional things that Moses did while a young prince of Egypt.

Moses commanded the Egyptian army in a campaign against the Ethiopians, who were plaguing the southern borders, that was so brilliant in its execution, and such an overwhelming victory, that they did not bother Egypt for generations.

Moses also engineered the building of one of Pharaoh's great cities. He made powerful and brilliant speeches to the court and to the people, and was revered as a god by the Egyptian populace.

By the time Moses reached the age of forty, he was a proven genius in several fields. Because of this, Pharaoh, who had no son of his own, chose him to be his successor over another member of the royal family.

So Moses grew up with all the vast treasures of Egypt at his disposal. All the comforts and pleasures of one of the greatest civilizations of all time were his to command.

Even today it is doubtful that any royalty could have such personal sensual pleasures and opulent creature comforts as those available to Moses.

MOSES' AMAZING DECISION

When we take all this into account, this statement concerning Moses' decision of faith becomes even more awesome:

By faith Moses, when he had become great, *refused* **to be called the son of Pharaoh's daughter;** *choosing* **rather to endure ill-treatment with the people of God, than to enjoy the passing pleasures of sin;** *considering* **reproach for the Messiah greater riches than**

**the treasures of Egypt; for HE WAS LOOKING TO
THE REWARD.** (Hebrews 11:24–26 HL)

There are several key points that must be observed to fully
understand the enormity of Moses' faith. The word usually
translated "grown up" in most Bibles is *ga`dal* in the origi-
nal Hebrew of Exodus 2:11, and is μέγας in the original
Greek. In both languages, the primary meaning is the same—
"to become great." The main point that the Holy Spirit is seeking to drive home is that Moses made his momentous decision
to follow God's call for his life when he was at the pinnacle of
human greatness and personal glory, not as a "down-and-
outer."

It is also important to understand that the action of the
main verb, **refused,** is preceded by the action of the two participles, **choosing** and **considering.** These two participles tell us
the mental process Moses went through to reach his decision
to refuse the throne of Egypt.

The first participle, **choosing,** contrasts the enormous difference between the two kinds of life involved in the choice.
On one side of the scale was the personal glory, power, wealth,
adulation, creature comforts, and security Moses had as prince
of Egypt. On the other side was the disgrace and degradation,
deprivation, humiliation, hardship, suffering, and danger of
identifying himself with the Israelite slaves.

It is also important to note that a man at forty years of age
is usually most vulnerable to the attacks of Satan. It is a time
when the male ego most needs reassurance. A time when security of career is most needed, when a man knows how to
enjoy pleasures and is most attached to them.

I'm sure Satan tempted Moses to view this situation from
the human viewpoint. Moses probably said to himself, "Why
should I leave all this and join with my people as a slave. After
all, when I become Pharaoh, I can help them more with my
position of power and authority."

But from God's divine viewpoint, He had a plan that
would only work if Moses left Egypt and the throne in order to
lead the Hebrews out of Egypt to the promised land. God's
plan rarely makes sense if we try to analyze it from the human
viewpoint, because we only have a limited perspective. God's

Spirit was working upon Moses to show him His perfect will. Moses didn't know the whole plan yet, but he knew enough about God to trust Him with the things he did not know.

So after carefully weighing the situation, Moses came to the conviction that suffering hardship in following God's plan was a much wiser investment than enjoying the pleasures of sin. The reason was: the enjoyment of sin was immediate, but temporary and fleeting; the enjoyment of God's reward was delayed, but eternal.

I'm sure that most of what is meant by "sin" here is not what would be considered immorality, but rather the greater and more difficult sins of pride, self-centeredness, and selfish ambition. All of these would have been a heady wine for someone in Moses' position.

The second participle, **considering,** indicates that Moses' choice was carefully and slowly made. On one side of his mind's scale of reason he put the tangible, visible, almost inconceivably vast treasures of Egypt. On the other side, the intangible promises of Israel's future kingdom with the Messiah. Moses chose the unseen future treasures of the Messiah's promised kingdom. The choice was clearly based on his trust in the trustworthiness of God's character. He was fully persuaded that what God promised, He was able and faithful to do.

What was the motivating secret behind Moses' humanly incredible choice? The Scripture tells us, **". . . for he looked away from all that would distract and kept focusing on the REWARD."** (This is the full meaning of the original Greek.)

Moses' choice perfectly demonstrates the Divine definition of faith. He truly was sure of what he hoped for and certain of things he could not see (Hebrews 11:1). It was his certainty that God cannot lie, and that He must keep His promises, that energized his decision.

SOURCE OF MOSES' KNOWLEDGE

What was the source of Moses' knowledge about Israel's destiny? Where did he get such an understanding and love for the Messiah, that it motivated him to lay aside the throne and all the treasures of Egypt to follow Him? It took a profound faith in the Messiah to plunge into such shame and suffering from such a lofty position.

As stated in the last chapter, I believe that Moses' mother and father taught him the promises given to Abraham, Isaac, and Jacob before he was finally given over to Pharaoh's daughter.

Moses surely was taught about Joseph's final promise and charge to the Israelites at his death.

Joseph's last testament of faith was this:

Then Joseph said to his brothers, "I am about to die. But God will surely come to your aid and take you up out of this land to the land He promised on oath to Abraham, Isaac and Jacob." And Joseph made the sons of Israel swear on oath and said, "God will surely come to your aid, and then you must carry my bones up from this place." So Joseph died at the age of a hundred and ten. And after they embalmed him, he was placed in a coffin in Egypt. (Genesis 50:24–26)

Joseph's ornate coffin was never buried, but kept in full view in the middle of the Israelite region. This was completely contrary to Egyptian custom. He had them do this so that every time someone would see the unburied coffin, it would be a reminder that Joseph believed in God's promise of sending a Deliverer. Joseph was also placed in God's hall of fame for this great act of faith in God's promise. Moses would surely have been aware of this strange means of reminding the people of God's promise.

It is certain that the Egyptian nation was acquainted with the Hebrew religion. After all, the Hebrews had been there for well over three hundred years. So it is reasonable to assume that their religious teachings were well known. Moses must have pursued the Divine revelation that was available, especially since he knew that he was of Hebrew descent, for the kind of faith Moses demonstrated would have taken years to develop.

The man who became Pharaoh as a consequence of

Moses' abdication grew up together with Moses in the royal court. This means that this future Pharaoh not only had available to him the same Divine revelations of Israel's God, but probably also discussed them as a boy with Moses. So when the Scripture says, "God hardened Pharaoh's heart," it was not without much prior striving with that same heart. Pharaoh had already hardened his heart against the LORD. The LORD just made it harder so that He could reveal Himself to the Egyptians through the mighty miraculous judgments that resulted from Pharaoh's obstinate refusal to let the Israelites go.

WHO WAS THE FOOL?

I'm sure that Moses' contemporaries thought he was a fool for turning down the throne and joining with a bunch of down and out slaves. But as we look back in history, how many have heard of Amunhotep II? Very few outside of scholars. This is the name of the Pharaoh believed to have inherited the throne. (He was the son of Thutmose III.)* But how many have heard of Moses? Even human history shows Moses to have been the wiser man. But what does eternity show?

In our day, when the emphasis is on instant gratification of our desires and the avoidance of hardships at any cost, this is a tremendously important lesson. Even within the evangelical church, some influential ministers have strayed from the Truth and are proclaiming a "health and wealth gospel." Some have dared to even teach that if you're not being financially blessed, it's because of a lack of faith or sin in your life. Perhaps these ministers would have counseled Moses "to stay with the treasures of Egypt and become Pharaoh, God doesn't want you to suffer and be poor!"

In His providence the LORD does make some wealthy, but not all. But those who seek after riches will fall into many snares. The Scripture says,

---

*Conservative scholars agree that Moses grew up in the Egyptian court under the reign of Thutmose III. It was he who chose Moses as his heir apparent over his own son. Amunhotep II became Pharaoh after Moses fled Egypt and his father died. He grew up under Moses' shadow and probably disliked him out of jealousy.

> But godliness actually is a means of great gain, when accompanied by contentment. For we have brought nothing into the world, so we cannot take anything out of it either. And if we have food and covering, with these we shall be content. But those who want to get rich fall into temptation and a snare and many foolish and harmful desires which plunge men into ruin and destruction. For the love of money is a root of all sorts of evil, and some by longing for it have wandered away from the faith, and pierced themselves with many a pang. (1 Timothy 6:6-10)

We need to have a sharp refocusing of our present life in the light of eternity and the promised rewards.

SETTLING THE QUESTION OF WHOSE WILL

Our heavenly Father calls upon each one of us to make a decision of faith about our lives. I am convinced that apart from this decision, we really don't begin to find God's plan for our lives. God says,

> Therefore, I urge you, brothers, in view of God's mercy, to offer your bodies as living sacrifices, holy and pleasing to God—this is your spiritual act of worship. Do not conform any longer to the pattern of this world, but be transformed by the renewing of your mind. Then you will be able to test and approve what God's will is—His good, pleasing and perfect will. (Romans 12:1-2)

Moses presented his body to God as a living sacrifice when he elected to follow what he knew of God's will and identified himself with the Hebrews. Moses chose God's plan for his life as final before he fully understood it. He believed on the basis of what he knew of God's love and mercy that He could be trusted to do the very best with his life in the unknown future.

Moses gave up what he could not keep to gain what he could not lose. This is a very essential part of true faith. Faith makes the thing promised for the future so real that the present can be sacrificed, if need be, for the better way.

The divine viewpoint of life says, **"For what is your life? It is even a vapor that appears for a little time and then vanishes away."** (James 4:14 NKJV) I heard a message once that compared the vapor trail left by a jet plane across the vastness of the sky to our lives. Each of us is blazing a vapor trail across the sky of time that appears for a little while and then vanishes. No one on earth will long remember our passing by—but God will. We can choose to leave a vapor trail during our short time on earth that will count for all eternity.

But it takes a decision, based on faith, to begin living for eternity. I learned a simple children's rhyme long ago that profoundly affected me:

> **Only one life,**
> **will soon be past;**
> **Only what is done for Christ**
> **will last.**

If you have never made a decisive decision to give God the title deed to your life, isn't it reasonable to do so? In the light of God's grace, we can trust Him to give our life the greatest meaning and fulfillment possible, and at the end it will have counted for eternity.

As you think over your life in the light of this chapter, whose example are you following, Amunhotep II's, or Moses'? Of these two, who was the fool? By faith, you can make a decision now that will count for all eternity.

CHAPTER SIX

God's B.D. Degree

For the eyes of the LORD range throughout the earth to strengthen those whose hearts are fully committed to Him.

2 Chronicles 16:9

After Moses' valiant decision to leave the royal court and follow God's call, he encountered some real problems. The LORD by this time had shown Moses that He was to be used to deliver the Israelites from their slavery as had been promised long before. This fact is brought out by the Holy Spirit through Stephen:

> **When Moses was forty years old, he decided to visit his fellow Israelites. He saw one of them being mistreated by an Egyptian, so he went to his defense and avenged him by killing the Egyptian. Moses thought that his own people would realize that God was using him to rescue them. . . .** (Acts 7:23–25)

But Moses did not know exactly how he was to deliver them, so in his spiritual immaturity he impetuously took matters into his own hands and sought to do the job in his own wisdom and strength. In other words, he operated by the human viewpoint.

This is the Old Testament account:

63

One day, after Moses had [become great], he went out to where his own people were and watched them at their hard labor. He saw an Egyptian beating a Hebrew, one of his own people. Glancing this way and that and seeing no one, he killed the Egyptian and hid him in the sand. The next day he went out and saw two Hebrews fighting. He asked the one in the wrong, "Why are you hitting your fellow Hebrew?"

The man said, "Who made you ruler and judge over us? Are you thinking of killing me as you killed the Egyptian?" Then Moses was afraid and thought, "What I did must have become known."

When Pharaoh heard of this, he tried to kill Moses, but Moses fled from Pharaoh and went to live in Midian. . . . (Exodus 2:11–15)

Humanly speaking, Moses had incredible talent, and was a trained warrior with great strength. The Egyptian taskmasters were all chosen because of their powerful builds, strength, and fighting ability. Yet Moses killed this one quickly, apparently with his bare hands.

However, this was not the plan God had in mind for delivering the Hebrews out of Egypt. With God, the end does not justify the means. Under Egyptian or any other law, this was murder, or manslaughter at the very least. It was not self-defense, nor was the Hebrew slave's life at stake. Moses simply got angry at the abusive treatment of one of his own race and killed the Egyptian.

Moses' heart was right but his method was wrong. God understood his righteous indignation, but couldn't approve his action.

I can't think of this without marveling at God's grace. We wouldn't see God's grace at work unless He was faithful to report the sins and failures of His greatest servants as well as their triumphs.

God saw that Moses' heart was fully committed to Him, and that he wanted to follow God's purpose for his life, which was to deliver Israel. But Moses did not yet know God's ways.

The worst thing that Moses did in this situation was to

operate on the basis of the human viewpoint (seeking to live for God through human talent, wisdom, and strength).

It is sometimes more difficult for a person like Moses to learn how to live by the Divine viewpoint because of his tremendous natural human abilities. Moses had to be taught that Israel could only be delivered by God's power, in God's time, and in God's way.

But isn't it beautiful that God deals with us on the basis of our present level of maturity. You wouldn't severely discipline a two-month-old baby for throwing his milk on the floor, but you would discipline a six year old.

DISCIPLINED BY GRACE

Moses was disciplined for killing the man and operating in the flesh, but in the process, God turned the discipline into blessing. The LORD promises, **"And we know that God causes ALL THINGS to work together for good to those who love God, to those who are called according to His purpose."** (Romans 8:28 NASB) Not all things are good. But God can cause all things, even our sins, to work together for good. It is this goodness of God that is designed to lead us to repentance so that we confess our sins and trust Him again. This is one of the most important promises in the whole Bible to learn and believe.

Some have disputed that this promise is applicable to all believers. Romans 8:28 is in a context that traces the sovereign work the LORD performs for each believer to bring him from God's election in the past into eternal glory in the future. Let me briefly trace the main points of this context.

The Holy Spirit sovereignly intercedes for each believer because we do not know how to pray as we ought. (Romans 8:26-27 NASB)

God sovereignly works all the circumstances together for good in the lives of those He calls (Romans 8:28), and even our love for Him is declared to be a gift of grace: **"In this is love, NOT that we loved God, but that He loved us and sent His Son to be the propitiation** [satisfaction of His justice] **for our sins."** (I John 4:10 NASB)

The LORD foreknew, predestined, called, justified, and glorified each believer in Christ (Romans 8:29–30). All of these things, from verses twenty-six through thirty, are presented as God's sovereign work, and are not based nor dependent on our merit. The rest of Romans chapter eight shows that nothing can unjustify the one whom God has justified. In fact, even God can't condemn the one for whom Christ has already been condemned on the cross. Nor can any created thing (which includes ourselves) separate us from the love of God that is secured through our union with Christ.

All of these truths were beautifully illustrated in the way God dealt with Moses. Even though Moses failed miserably, we surely can't say that "he was the bird with the broken wing that would never fly as high again," can we? The grace of God delights in changing great sinners into great saints. That way, there is no argument about who gets the glory.

THE FLIGHT INTO BOOTCAMP

It is interesting to note that the only one who could have gotten Moses into trouble for killing the taskmaster was the very Hebrew whom Moses rescued. No one else but he saw what happened; the text specifically says that Moses carefully checked to see if anyone was around before he killed the Egyptian.

Most ministers know that sometimes the person you try to help the most will turn and do you the greatest harm. Instead of this Hebrew being grateful, he spread the news, knowing that it would get Moses into severe trouble. He was probably envious of Moses' exalted position.

Human nature doesn't change. Christians are very slow to learn that there are some things that, even if true, are better kept quiet. (I am not suggesting we ought to cover up a crime, but you see what I'm getting at.) The LORD says, **"He who covers over an offense promotes love, but whoever repeats the matter separates close friends."** (Proverbs 17:9) In other words, if it doesn't specifically edify, shut up. God hates gossip and the sowing of discord among the brethren (Proverbs 6:16–19).

Even though Moses was the favored prince, the Pharaoh had a violent reaction to his deed. The reason behind this is clear. Pharaoh was already afraid of the Hebrew people. He saw in Moses' act that he was more loyal to his own blood than to his adopted parents. With someone like Moses to lead the Hebrews, Pharaoh must have reasoned, anything could happen. He saw Moses as a dangerous and ungrateful traitor to the royal family and Egypt, and therefore pronounced the death penalty on him. But Moses was already fleeing the country by the time the soldiers sought him.

HOW GOD TURNED FAILURE INTO BLESSING

Once again we see the grace of God in action. Notice carefully God's commendation of Moses in His hall of fame, **"By faith he [Moses] left Egypt, not fearing the king's anger; he persevered because he saw Him who is invisible."** (Hebrews 11:27)

A fantastic truth emerges: God says that when we repent and confess our sins, He not only forgives them, but He doesn't remember them or hold them against us. Just look at this commendation. There is no mention of Moses' sin of killing the Egyptian, which caused the flight into the desert. Nor is there any mention of the fact that at first he was afraid and fled from Pharaoh.

All God remembers is Moses' faith, which caused him to seek to deliver Israel. Remembered also is Moses' faith as he trusted God moment by moment to sustain and protect him in the trackless wasteland of the scorching Sinai desert. These principles are in accordance with the following promises:

If we CONFESS our sins, He is faithful and righteous to forgive us our sins and to cleanse us from all unrighteousness. (1 John 1:9 NASB)

He who conceals his sins does not prosper, but whoever CONFESSES and renounces them finds mercy. (Proverbs 28:13)

Then I ACKNOWLEDGED my sin to You
and DID NOT COVER UP my iniquity.
I said, "I will CONFESS
my transgressions to the LORD—and You forgave
the guilt of my sin. (Psalm 32:5)

> I, even I, am He who blots out
> your transgressions, for My own sake,
> and remembers your sins no more.
> (Isaiah 43:25)

I have wiped out your transgressions like a thick
cloud, and your sins like a heavy mist. Return to
Me, for I have redeemed you. (Isaiah 44:22 NASB)

> If you, O LORD, kept a record of sins,
> O LORD, who could stand?
> But with You there is forgiveness;
> therefore You are feared [reverently trusted].
> I wait for the LORD, my soul waits,
> and in HIS WORD I put my hope. (Psalm
> 130:3–5)

This is a preview of what it will be like at the judgment
seat of Christ and in Heaven. Our LORD Jesus and our heavenly Father will only commend and reward us for the things
we did by faith with the right motive through the power of the
Holy Spirit. The rest will be burned up and forgotten. I'm convinced the Father is going to brag about His kid's acts of faith
for all eternity. According to the Bible, believing God is the
greatest gift we humans can give Him.

GOD'S FORTY-YEAR SEMINARY

Moses, weary and confused about his future, fled to the
land of Midian, which generally covered the area on both sides
of what is known today as the Gulf of Aqaba. This included
both the east coast of the Sinai peninsula and the west coast of
Arabia, where there was a wild and vast land inhabited by

bedouins (meaning "sons of the desert") who lived the no-madic life of shepherds.

Nice Going God!

I am sure that Moses felt that he had blown it so badly that God had no more purpose for his life. He may have even been feeling a little self-pity and some frustration with the LORD. He probably thought something like this: "After all, LORD, I gave up everything to follow you. Then when I make my first move to deliver Your people, You let all hell break loose. Now I have no throne and no more purpose in Your plan, no country, no family, and I'm broke. Nice going God, it really pays to serve You."

The Holy Spirit gives us these brief details of what happened:

> . . . **Moses fled from Pharaoh and went to live in Midian, where he sat down by a well. Now a priest of Midian had seven daughters, and they came to draw water and fill the troughs to water their father's flock. Some shepherds came along and drove them away, but Moses got up and came to their rescue and watered their flock.** [This once again confirms that Moses must have been a powerful man and a real warrior.]
>
> **When the girls returned to Reuel their father, he asked them, "Why have you returned so early today?"**
>
> **They answered, "An Egyptian rescued us from the shepherds. He even drew water for us and watered the flock."**
>
> **"And where is he?" he asked his daughters. "Why did you leave him? Invite him to have something to eat."**
>
> **Moses agreed to stay with the man, who gave his daughter Zipporah to Moses in marriage. Zipporah gave birth to a son, and Moses named him Gershom, saying, "I have become an alien in a [strange] land."** (Exodus 2:15–22)

Looking from the Divine viewpoint, the LORD had graciously provided a new family in a secure place for Moses so that his spiritual training could be accomplished. The priest of Midian was a true believer in the God of Abraham, Isaac, and Jacob.

GOD'S GRACIOUS PROVIDENCE

It is amazing Divine providence that led Moses to the tent of the priest of Midian, who became Moses' father-in-law and friend. The priest is called **Reuel** in Exodus 2:18. But he is called **Jethro** in Exodus 18. When I carefully searched out why, the LORD showed me a precious insight.

Reuel is actually the tribal name from which Jethro is descended. The forefather of the tribe was the second born of the five sons of **Esau** (who was Jacob's unbelieving twin brother). Reuel's mother, **Basemath,** was the daughter of **Ishmael** (the father of the Arab nations), who was the half brother of **Isaac.** The important point is this: out of all of Esau's five sons, only Reuel's name indicates a relationship with God. Reuel means "companion of God." Jethro is directly descended from this godly line. This explains why he is called the *priest* of Midian.

Now look at the providential grace of God. The LORD put Moses under the care of one of the few true believers in the world outside of the Israelites who were still in Egypt. And to top it all, they were distant relatives. He gave Moses his oldest daughter, Zipporah ("a beautiful bird," in Hebrew), as his wife.

We learn from Exodus chapter 18 that Jethro was a Godly and wise man who loved the LORD. I'm sure that he helped Moses to learn quietly much more about the God of his fathers.

The name that Moses gave his first son reveals a great deal about how he felt about himself and his future at that time. The name Gershom, which means "an alien in a strange land," suggests that Moses was feeling forlorn and sorry for himself, not yet recognizing what God's grace had done. Moses was still operating in the human viewpoint. He apparently had not yet conquered his pride in having been a royal figure whose exploits had shaken the very center of power, civilization, culture, and education. It was hard for him to accept being a foreigner in the backside of the desert, out of the mainstream of world events, and not even the head of his own family.

Moses had a second son during this time. He would probably have been born some three to four years after Moses arrived in Midian. His second son's name is very important because it reveals that by that time Moses was beginning to see the Divine viewpoint of life, especially that aspect that says that God never allows anything to happen in a believer's life by accident. If we trust Him, everything will work together for our good. The Scripture says about the second son's name, **". . . and the other [son] was named Eliezer, for he [Moses] said, 'My father's God was my helper; He saved me from the sword of Pharaoh.'"** (Exodus 18:4) The meaning of this name indicates that Moses had a real change of perspective concerning God and his circumstances. He apparently had begun to recognize God's gracious care for him, and His providential arrangement of circumstances for his best good.

THE LOST FORTY YEARS

Very little is revealed about the forty years Moses spent in the backside of the desert; we can only seek to read between the lines. But God revealed enough to throw a strong focus on the most essential elements of Moses' faith-training.

The life of a bedouin has changed very little from Moses' time until this day. It is simple, rugged, and basic. The bedouin moves with the seasons in order to keep his flocks of sheep, goats, and camels in the best areas for water and food. Everything he has is carried from place to place on his camels or donkeys. His palace is his tent, and it can be made remarkably comfortable and beautiful.

A wealthy sheikh (a tribal chief) of Moses' day would have his tent floors covered with beautiful hand-woven rugs. His rooms were divided by ornately woven tapestry hangings. The key to everything, however, was portability.

The most important time of day for the bedouin is the evening meal. After the hot desert sun goes down, when the work is done and the evening cools, he gathers his family about him and they share the principal meal of the day. It is generally at this time that the bedouin, who loves to talk about everything, speaks of the latest news, tells entertaining stories, and discusses God and His ways.

The bedouin sheikh, which is what Jethro was, is the absolute ruler and authority of his tribe. His word is law. Life and death depend on his judgment.

But as the priest of Midian, Jethro had spiritual authority over the other sheikhs of Midian as well. In his position as sheikh and priest, Jethro had authority over Moses also. He and Moses must have spent many thousands of hours discussing the God of Abraham, who was their common forefather and spiritual ideal.

A LESSON IN SOLITUDE

Moses became a shepherd for his father-in-law. This was the lowest of all occupations in the estimation of the Egyptian culture. So this was an extremely humbling job for a former prince and the heir apparent to the throne of Pharaoh.

As a shepherd, Moses would have spent many days at a time in the solitude of the desert wilderness. I have been in this area and it's awesome. The strange beauty of the rose-colored mountains of Edom by the deep azure blue of the Gulf of Aqaba, the stark majesty of the rose-pink granite mountains of the Sinai, struck me with wonder, as I am sure they did Moses some thirty-five hundred years before. It's the only place I've ever been where the silence is so intense it can be felt. So many stars are visible at night that one can't help but meditate on the power and wonder of the God who created them. In this type of setting, it's easy to understand how David must have felt when he, as a young teenage shepherd boy alone in the wilderness of Judah, meditated upon the stars and wrote, **"The heavens declare the glory of God; the firmament shows His handiwork."** (Psalm 19:1 NKJV)

THE PRINCIPLE OF BROKEN THINGS

Surely Moses meditated about God during those simple, quiet days with nature. After forty years, the pomp and glory of his earlier days, the complexity of Egyptian civilization, the business of royal life, the intricacies of court society, the exaltation of being a prince, the cocky confidence of being highly educated and an accomplished genius, were by now dim memories. By this time, Moses had lost all thoughts of grandeur. He certainly felt that the lofty calling of being Israel's Deliverer was forfeited long ago.

He was now content to be simply a member of the LORD's people and a subordinate member of priest Jethro's family. The Egyptian world had long since written Moses off and forgotten him—but not the LORD. The LORD had at last prepared Moses for the final phase of training for his mission, for the LORD says, **"My power is made perfect in weakness."** This means that God's power is set free to work without hindrance through the one who realizes that he is too weak in his human ability to accomplish God's will. Great faith only becomes possible after God teaches us this lesson. However, the Holy Spirit doesn't break our spirits so that we are without a sense of worth or confidence. He simply transfers our confidence from ourselves to God and convinces us that He will work His mighty power and wisdom through us. Our faith then begins to grab hold of promises like this: **"Behold, I am the LORD, the God of all flesh; is anything too difficult for Me?"** (Jeremiah 32:27 NASB) We begin to realize that we can do all that God calls us to do, because our faith in Him releases His power to accomplish it.

The metal of Moses' character at eighty years of age was now tempered in the furnace of God's training school, and was ready to be poured into the mold of God's purpose. Without erasing the human talent and training, the LORD had now forged Moses into the kind of person who could be taught how to believe Him on the basis of His promises alone.

ANOTHER BROKEN VESSEL

The principle of God breaking our confidence in the flesh is so important that He gives us another supreme example in the New Testament. Saul of Tarsus, who became the great apostle Paul, gives a startling illustration of this principle in his own testimony:

> **If anyone else has a mind to put confidence in the flesh, I have far more [reason]: circumcised the eighth day, of the nation of Israel, of the tribe of Benjamin, a Hebrew of Hebrews; as to the Law, a Pharisee; as to zeal, a persecutor of the church; as to the righteousness which is in the Law, found BLAMELESS.**
>
> **But whatever things were gain to me, those things I have counted as loss for the sake of Christ. More than that, I count all things to be loss in view of the surpassing value of knowing Christ Jesus my LORD, for whom I have suffered the loss of all things, and count them but rubbish in order that I may gain Christ, and may be found in Him, not having a righteousness of my own derived from the Law, but that which is through faith in Christ, the righteousness which comes from God on the basis of faith.** (Philippians 3:4–9 NASB)

This testimony shows Paul to be the best example of a man who tried to gain God's acceptance by his own human performance. Under Divine inspiration he said of himself,

> **Here is a trustworthy saying that deserves full acceptance: Christ Jesus came into the world to save sinners—OF WHOM I AM THE WORST. But for that very reason I was shown mercy so that in me, the WORST OF SINNERS, Christ Jesus might display His unlimited patience as an example for those**

who would believe on Him and receive eternal life.
(1 Timothy 1:15-16)

But why does the Holy Spirit call Paul the worst sinner of all time? Was it because he killed Christians? Nero, Stalin, and Mao Tse-dung, to name a few, all massacred more Christians than Paul. No, it wasn't for any of the usual reasons most Christians think. Paul was the worst sinner who ever lived because he was the most religious. This is his point in the Philippians passage quoted above. Religion can be defined as trying to earn God's acceptance by human merits. The person who does this more than any other, treads under foot the blood of Christ and says that it is not sufficient to save him.

The application to us today should be obvious. God has always worked the same way through His servants. If you wish to be used effectively by the LORD, then you must come to that point where you realize that nothing in you can accomplish God's plan. The only way to serve God is to see the challenges of living and serving Him in the light of His ability to work through you by His Spirit. In this way, **"we cease from our own labors as God** [on the seventh day of creation] **did from His, and enter His Rest."** (Hebrews 4:10 HL.)

PRINCIPLES OF GOD'S B.D. DEGREE

Nothing more in the Bible is mentioned concerning the life of Moses during the forty years of his life in Midian. There are some important lessons to deduce from this.

First, no one, no matter how talented or spiritually gifted, is ready to be used of God until he learns how to live by the Divine viewpoint of life. He has to be able to consistently approach each challenge on the basis of God's ability to deal with it through him. Moses, in his immature zeal, tried to accomplish God's ministry with his enormous human talent. *But it set him back 40 years in God's plan.*

Second, God puts a premium on the preparation of a servant, and he doesn't rush or cut it short. Many Christian leaders today play down the importance of training in systematic theology and Bible exposition. As a result, we have Christians seeking to lead who are themselves "carried about by every wind of doctrine." Now I am quick to agree that a theological training alone isn't enough. We also have to be filled with the Spirit and know how to enter God's rest by faith. The issue is not either-or, but both-and.

The filling of the Spirit without biblical grounding can lead to fanatical practices and doctrinal errors. A theological training without the filling of the Spirit leads to unloving spiritual deadness and ineffective ministry.

When a person graduates today from most seminaries, he is given a B.D. degree, which means "Bachelor of Divinity." God has much greater degrees that He requires of His servants. One is the B.A. degree, which means we must be "born again." The other is God's B.D. degree, which means "backside of the desert" training.

God's greatest servants had these two degrees. Abraham spent many years living out in the desert in tents before he finally learned to believe God's promises.

Moses spent forty years earning his backside-of-the-desert degree before he was broken of self-confidence and taught God-confidence.

David, the man after God's own heart, spent many years going through trials in the backside of the desert before he was made king of Israel.

Jesus spent thirty years in obscurity preparing for a three-year ministry, but He turned the world around in those three years. (If even the Son of God needed that kind of preparation, what should it tell us?)

Saul of Tarsus was allowed only a little taste of ministry before God whisked him off into the desert of Arabia for a few years. He emerged later as Paul the Apostle. And it is important to remember also that Paul knew the Hebrew Scriptures by memory before he was born again.

All of this indicates that no matter how spiritually gifted a person may be, he or she must have training and experience to mature into a truly anointed and productive minister.

On this subject, the LORD says to those who would be His servant,

Study to show yourself approved of God, a workman who doesn't need to be ashamed and who handles correctly the WORD OF TRUTH . . . But as for you [Timothy], continue in what you have learned and have become convinced of, because you know those from whom you learned it, and how from infancy you have KNOWN THE HOLY SCRIPTURES, which are able to make you wise for salvation through faith in Christ Jesus. ALL SCRIPTURE IS GOD-BREATHED and is useful for teaching, rebuking, correcting and training in righteousness, so that the man of God may be thoroughly equipped for every good work. (2 Timothy 2:15 HL; 3:14–17)

This Scripture was written specifically for the prophetic time in which we are living. How I pray that all of us will take it to heart.

Third, the fact that it took God so long to prepare Moses indicates how difficult it is for a greatly talented and accomplished person to learn how to stop trying to operate in the HVP and to start living by the DVP. I remember when I was in Campus Crusade for Christ the idea was given that if we could just win to Christ Mr. Top-Man-on-Campus, we would have such a great ready-made witness. Such a person can become useful, but not before he gets broken of the HVP. Frequently, some of the most unlikely students became the greatest disciples. (The reason is that they already knew that they had to walk by faith. Looking at life from the Divine viewpoint is an acquired skill of seeing every situation through the eyes of faith—it is a way of seeing God as bigger than our problems. Pride is the great enemy of the DVP. One has to have true humility to live by it.)

A DIFFERENT KIND OF MAN

When Moses came to Midian, he was a physically robust, forty-year-old man who was at the peak of his capabilities both physically and mentally. As we have seen, he was one of the most highly trained, intelligent, talented, and accomplished human beings in history.

The Moses we meet in the next chapter is very different—he is now a man specially trained of God to do the impossible. At eighty years old, Moses received his B.D. degree, and he had begun to learn about "combat faith."

CHAPTER SEVEN

Power Perfected
in Weakness

**But the LORD said to me, "My GRACE is sufficient
for you, for MY power is made perfect in weakness."
That is why, for Christ's sake, I delight in weak-
nesses, in insults, in hardships, in persecutions, in
difficulties. For when I realize I am weak, then I am
truly strong.**

2 Corinthians 12:8,10 HL

GOD RE-CALLS HIS CHAMPION

At the end of these forty years of passive resignation to his
lot in life, with no thought of ever being used by the LORD in
any great way, an extraordinary thing happened to Moses. The
Word of God reports this holy moment as follows:

**Now Moses was tending the flock of Jethro his
father-in-law, the Priest of Midian, and he led the
flock to the far side of the desert and came to Horeb,
the mountain of God. There the Angel of the LORD
appeared to him in flames of fire from within a
bush. Moses saw that though the bush was on fire it
did not burn up. So Moses thought, "I will go over**

and see this strange sight—why the bush does not burn up."

When the LORD saw that he had gone over to look, God called to him from within the bush, "Moses! Moses!" And Moses said, "Here I am."

"Do not come any closer," God said. "Take off your sandals, for the place where you are standing is holy ground." Then He said, "I Am the God of your father, the God of Abraham, the God of Isaac and the God of Jacob." At this, Moses hid his face, because he was afraid to look at God. (Exodus 3:1-6)

How unexpected this sacred appointment was. Moses was casually guiding his flock to wherever the water and food was plentiful, as he had done for decades. In this area, there are millions of little dry shrubs that are highly flammable. Suddenly Moses sees one of these bushes with flames shooting forth from within, yet not consumed.

Completely unaware of the greater significance of the phenomenon, Moses' curiosity is aroused and he walks over to investigate.

Can you imagine the incredible shock to Moses when God's voice boomed out from within the flaming bush? There is no indication that God ever spoke directly to Moses before this. But now, at the most unexpected time, when Moses had resigned himself to finish out his life in obscurity, the LORD appeared and spoke directly to him. God's ways are strange and wonderful.

ANY OLD BUSH WILL DO, MOSES!

I once heard a great British Bible teacher named Major Ian Thomas comment on this passage. He noted that Moses was taught a great spiritual lesson even by the method God chose to get his attention. The lesson was this: out of all the common bushes of that desert, one became eternally significant.

The LORD demonstrated to Moses that *any old bush—as long as it's available—will do to manifest His glory*. This bush was no different from any one of the thousands of others in the area—except for one thing; God chose to engulf it with His presence and power.

God's Glory in Earthen Vessels

The LORD Jesus taught this same kind of lesson in John chapter two. When the wedding feast ran out of wine, He took six common earthen water vessels that were overlooked by others and had them filled with water. Then He miraculously changed the water to the best aged wine. In this miracle, the LORD Jesus illustrated that any old earthen vessel will do to manifest God's glory—as long as it is available and clean. Water was a symbol of the Holy Spirit, the earthen vessels were symbols of our human bodies, and wine was a symbol of joy produced by the Holy Spirit.

The LORD does the same with these human vessels of ours—as long as we are *clean* and *available*. God summarizes this principle through Paul: **"But we have this treasure in [earthen vessels] to show that this all-surpassing power is from God and not from us."** (2 Corinthians 4:7 HL)

MOSES! MOSES!

Whenever God spoke to a servant in the Old Testament and repeated his name twice, it meant that he had matured. This was a commonly understood practice in that time. For instance, when Abraham, in total faith-obedience, was about to offer his beloved son Isaac to the LORD as a burnt sacrifice, the LORD called out to him, **"'Abraham, Abraham! . . . Do not lay a hand on the boy . . . Do not do anything to him. Now I know that you fear God, because you have not withheld from Me your son, your only son.'"** (Genesis 22:11–12) The LORD also repeated Jacob's name twice when He told him not to be afraid to go down to Egypt. (Genesis 46:1–7) The repeating of Moses' name indicates that he too had become mature in God's estimation.

What had started off for Moses as a simple pursuit of curiosity, ended up being a life-changing encounter with the eternal God.

The LORD reveals Himself to Moses in a special way just as He had done previously to Abraham and Jacob. The LORD said to him, **"Moses! Moses! . . . I am the God of your father, the God of Abraham, the God of Isaac and the God of Jacob."** Jesus later quoted this same verse as proof of the resurrection. God used a grammatical construction in Hebrew that means "a continuous state of being." Since God told Moses that He continued to be **(I am)** the God of his dead forefathers, Abraham, Isaac, and Jacob, they must have been alive with God. (Jesus interpreted it this way to the Jewish religious leaders of His day: **"But about the resurrection of the dead—have you not read what God said to you, 'I am the God of Abraham, the God of Isaac, and the God of Jacob'? He is not the God of the dead but of the living."** (Matthew 22:31–32)) Moses must have been thrilled by the original revelation. (Incidentally, Jesus quotes this Old Testament passage and says that it is what GOD SAID TO THEM, thus showing His view of the Divine origin, preservation, and authority of the Scriptures.)

The LORD continued to speak to Moses out of the flaming bush and said,

> **I have indeed seen the misery of My people in Egypt. I have heard them crying out because of their slave drivers, and I am concerned about their suffering. So I HAVE COME DOWN TO RESCUE THEM from the hand of the Egyptians and to bring them up out of that land into a good and spacious land, a land flowing with milk and honey—the home of the Canaanites, Hittites, Amorites, Perizzites, Hivites and Jebusites. And now the cry of the Israelites has reached Me, and I have seen the way the Egyptians are oppressing them.** (Exodus 3:7–9)

MOSES TRIES TO "CHICKEN OUT"

Up until this point, Moses must have been listening with unbridled enthusiasm. He was probably saying to himself, "Yea, God! Way to go, LORD! Give those dirty Egyptians what

82

they deserve. Go get 'em, LORD!" But when the LORD said the following, Moses quickly sobered up: **"So now, GO. I AM SENDING *YOU* TO PHARAOH to bring My people the Israelites out of Egypt."** (Exodus 3:10)

"I beg your pardon, LORD," Moses must have thought, "**WHO** did you say you're sending?" The Scripture says, **"But Moses said to God, 'Who am I, that I should go to Pharaoh and bring the Israelites out of Egypt?"** (Exodus 3:11)

What a different man Moses has become. No longer is he the brash, cocksure young man who thought he was God's gift to the Israelites. Now he has been humbled to such a degree that he is almost *too* lacking in confidence. Moses was probably thinking, "No thanks, LORD. I've already tried that program once. Those stiff-necked people double-crossed me and almost got me killed. I don't want to try to lead that rebellious bunch again."

Then the LORD gave a promise to Moses that should have ended all of his hesitancy: **"I WILL BE WITH YOU."** (Exodus 3:12)

But instead, Moses began a long series of objections and excuses that reflected a severe lapse of confidence.

Excuse No. 1: "I Don't Know Your Name"

"Moses said to God, 'Suppose I go to the Israelites and say to them, "The God of your fathers has sent me to you," and they ask me, "What is his name?" Then what shall I tell them?'" (Exodus 3:13)

The LORD answers with a new revelation of Himself: **"God said to Moses, 'I am who I am. This is what you are to say to the Israelites: "*I AM* has sent me . . ."'"** (Exodus 3:14) This great and holy name means, among other things, sovereign, eternal self-existence. The anglicized word for the Hebrew "I Am" is "Jehovah." It is considered so holy by the Israelites that they will not pronounce it, but instead they substitute the name "Adonai."

The LORD went on to instruct Moses about calling together the Hebrew elders and what to say to them. Of special significance is God's prophetic warning that Pharaoh would not let the Israelites go until He judged him with many mighty signs and wonders.

Excuse No. 2: "What If the Israelites Don't Believe That God Sent Me?"

Moses could still remember how difficult it was to convince the Hebrews about Divine deliverance. So his objection had some basis in reality. The LORD showed Moses two miraculous signs to perform before the elders of Israel. One was to turn his staff into a snake, the other was to make his hand leperous and then heal it. The LORD promised him that the two signs would convince the elders of his Divine mission.

Excuse No. 3: "I Am Not Eloquent"

One can hardly recognize this new Moses! **"Moses said to the LORD, 'O LORD, I have never been eloquent, neither in the past nor since you have spoken to your servant. I am slow of speech and tongue.'"** (4:10) Moses was really grasping for reasons not to go back to Egypt. As a matter of fact, remember what the Holy Spirit said about Moses through Stephen: **"Moses was educated in all the wisdom of the Egyptians and was powerful in SPEECH and action."** (Acts 7:22) If Moses was slow of speech, it must have been a recent development.

But note the grace and gentleness of the Almighty God as He continues to reason with Moses and give him promise after promise in answer to his efforts to back out.

"The LORD said to him, 'Who gave man his mouth? Who makes him deaf or mute? Who gives him sight or makes him blind? Is it not I, the LORD? Now GO; I WILL . . . teach you what to say.'" (Exodus 4:11)

Soon after first learning about being filled with the Holy Spirit, I was asked to teach a Bible class. This immediately created a dilemma for me. I had always had such terrible stage fright that even the thought of speaking before a group of people was terrifying. I quit a speech class at the University of

Houston because I had been petrified with fear while attempting to give a speech. By faith I agreed to do it, even though every part of my being wanted to say no.

Then I went through an intense battle as I sought to prepare and believe the LORD for a "miraculous healing." As I prayed and searched the Scriptures for a promise of strength, the LORD led me to this passage. I was immediately encouraged as the Holy Spirit gave me assurance that God can even make the dumb speak. I claimed this promise and with trembling knees got up to teach. To my amazement, from the time I opened my mouth the fear left. From that experience until now, I always claim a promise before getting up to speak. In the many difficult speaking situations I've had since, the LORD has always answered my faith and given me His ability to communicate.

How did Moses receive this magnificent personal promise? You know, I have always been encouraged by Moses' response, because it gives me assurance that my own lapses into unbelief will not negate the faithfulness and patience of the LORD. (Also note for reference in chapter sixteen on why Christians suffer that God says He is ultimately responsible for a person being blind, deaf, or dumb.)

Just look at Moses' reply—and remember, he was talking directly with God: **"But Moses said, 'O LORD, please send someone else to do it.'"** (Exodus 4:13)

The Bible frequently reveals that the LORD has a great sense of humor. We see this demonstrated again in His response to Moses' unbelief: **"Then the LORD's anger burned against Moses and He said, 'What about your brother, Aaron the Levite? I know he can speak well.'"** (Exodus 4:14) This was humorous sarcasm on the LORD's part. Aaron wasn't educated and he couldn't speak well at all. Moses was probably ten times better a speaker, especially in the Egyptian language. But as a result of Moses' reluctance to trust, the LORD made Moses tell Aaron what to say, and then Aaron spoke on Moses' behalf to Pharaoh. I'm sure this arrangement later became very awkward and frustrating for Moses, and he surely must have lived to regret his excuses.

At the very time this Divine encounter was going on, the LORD had Aaron well on his way to meet his brother Moses.

The LORD had somehow miraculously revealed to him not only that Moses was alive, but where to find him.

LORD, I BELIEVE; HELP MY UNBELIEF!

Moses began to believe the LORD. He went to his father-in-law and requested permission to return to Egypt and check on the status of his people. (Moses had to ask permission because Jethro was over him in authority. It also showed his respect for Jethro.)

KEEPING A COVENANT AND BUSTING A MARRIAGE

Moses took Zipporah and his two sons with him, but along the way a very strange thing happened: **"At a lodging place on the way, the LORD met Moses and was about to kill him. But Zipporah took a flint knife, cut off her sons' foreskins and threw them at Moses' feet. 'Surely you are a bloody bridegroom to me,' she said. So the LORD let him alone."** [When she said 'bloody bridegroom,' she was referring to circumcision.] (Exodus 4:24–26 HL)

This incident was the end of Moses and Zipporah's marriage. It appears that Zipporah was the reason why Moses had not obeyed the LORD and circumcised his sons, because she expressed anger and contempt for this divinely instituted ritual. She also insulted Moses when she called him a bloody husband and threw their son's foreskins at his feet.

The LORD held Moses accountable for allowing his wife to sway him from keeping His most solemn covenant with Israel. Concerning circumcision,

> **God said to Abraham . . . "This is My covenant with you and your descendants after you for the generations to come. You are to undergo circumcision, and it will be THE SIGN of the covenant between Me and you. For the generations to come EVERY MALE among you who is eight days old must be circumcised, including those who are not your offspring.**

Whether born in your household or bought with money, they must be circumcised. My covenant in your flesh is to be an EVERLASTING COVENANT. Any uncircumcised male, who has not been circumcised in the flesh, will be CUT OFF from his people; he has broken My covenant." (Genesis 17:10–14 HL)

This incident shows us that even when we have been divinely called, we can't set about to do God's work and fail to keep certain fundamental commands of His Word that have to do with basic obedience. Moses was taking his sons to be part of Israel's community and to share in their covenant with the LORD. So at this point, the command of circumcision had to be obeyed. Moses had failed to believe God and keep the covenant of circumcision.

It was for this reason that the LORD met Moses on the way to Egypt and apparently so afflicted him with a sickness that he couldn't get out of bed to do the circumcision himself, so he ordered his wife to do it. If she had not obeyed, he would have died.

This issue caused such a controversy that Moses had to let Zipporah and his sons go back to her father. The Scripture says, **"After Moses had sent away his wife Zipporah, his father-in-law Jethro received her and her two sons."** (Exodus 18:2)

A few years later Moses married a Cushite woman. The Cushites are descended from Cush, the father of all the black races. In fact *cush* means "black." Moses was severely criticized for his remarriage, especially to a non-Israelite, by his sister Miriam, and by Aaron.

The LORD ended that little gossip campaign by smiting Miriam with leprosy until Moses prayed for her healing (see Numbers 12:10–15). I think the many in the Church who love to gossip and criticize would profit greatly by taking heed of this passage. It also teaches us that the LORD is absolutely opposed to any form of racial prejudice for any reason! Moses' second wife was definitely black.

Many in the Church today teach that divorce and remarriage disqualifies a person from the LORD's service. What about Moses? He killed a man, divorced, and remarried. I'm not trying to minimize sin. I'm only seeking to maximize God's forgiving and restoring power through His grace. Divorce is a sin, but not an unforgivable sin. If God could and did forgive this sin under the age of Law, is it not possible for Him to forgive the same under the age of Grace? If God doesn't forgive sin, then we are all in the wrong vocation anyway, aren't we?

There are many wounded and battered people in the Church today who, because they have been divorced and remarried, are given the idea that repentance and forgiveness just don't apply to them. They are consigned to perpetual mediocrity and second-class citizenship in the Church community. They often miss out on God's true calling for their lives because they listen to their neighbor's judgmental spirit, rather than to God's word. Thank God Moses didn't believe his brother and sister's legalistic attack, or we would have a completely different Bible.

A COMFORTING REUNION

After Moses' wife left, the LORD comforted him by the arrival of his brother Aaron. The two brothers returned to Egypt together to take on Pharaoh and the Hebrew elders in the name of the LORD.

Moses showed the Hebrew elders the signs the LORD had given, and they believed and accepted him. When the people heard that the LORD was concerned about them and their misery, they all bowed their heads and worshiped. The stage was now set for Moses to learn how God's power could work through him.

CHAPTER EIGHT

How Faith Humbled
an Empire

God is opposed to the proud, but gives grace to the
humble . . . he who humbles himself shall be exalted
. . . before honor comes humility.
James 4:6; Luke 14:11; Proverbs 15:33 NASB

THE MOSES WHO RETURNED

The LORD was now finished with the initial phase of
Moses' training. The key to the great things He was about to
do through Moses was now in place. The Holy Spirit testified
about the importance of this key to Moses' spiritual success:
**"Now Moses was a VERY HUMBLE man, more humble than
anyone else on the face of the earth."** (Numbers 12:3) True
humility is one of the characteristics God cherishes most in a
man, and it is always prominent in the one He greatly uses.

Incidentally, true humility is not going around telling people how worthless you are, or making a big deal out of saying
that there is nothing good in you. No! A truly humble person
has a sense of self-worth because of the new nature God created in His own image within him through the miracle of the
new birth. The humble person simply accepts with thanksgiving what God has made him.

True humility is to recognize and appreciate the new person God has created you to be, to enjoy the deeds that God does through you, but to know that you never deserved these things and you never will. It is recognizing that everything is done by God's grace.

John the Baptist beautifully demonstrated true humility when his disciples tried to promote a competition between him and Jesus. They were disturbed because Jesus was baptizing *more* converts than he was. But John replied, **"A man can receive nothing, unless it has been given him from heaven. . . . He** [Jesus] **must increase, but I must decrease."** (John 3:27, 30 NASB)

The humble person does not compete with other people for attention, or to be recognized as the greatest servant of God, or the most "spiritual" person in the group. He relaxes and lets God exalt him if that is His will. He competes only with himself to fulfill the race God has set for him. The Lord Jesus Christ expressed God's attitude on this principle· **'For whoever exalts himself will be humbled, and whoever humbles himself will be exalted."** (Matthew 23:12) The LORD promises, **"Humility and fear of [reverence for] the LORD bring wealth and honor and life."** (Proverbs 22:4)

It was a truly humble Moses who went before Pharaoh by faith and in the LORD's name asked the king to let the people of Israel go. He was now confident in the LORD's ability and not in his own. Moses knew that God had sent him on a specific mission, and had promised to totally supply the power to accomplish it.

MOSES' FIRST CONFRONTATION WITH PHARAOH

Looking at it from the human viewpoint, the first encounter with Pharaoh was an unmitigated disaster. When Moses asked the king to let the people go sacrifice to the LORD, Pharaoh not only made fun of the Hebrews' God, but drastically increased their work load. Because of this, the elders of Israel became furious at Moses and Aaron and said, **"May the LORD look upon you and judge you! You have made us a** stench to Pharaoh and his officials and have put a sword in their hand to kill us." (Exodus 5:21)

One of the first principles in learning to crack the faith barrier and entering the sphere of combat faith is that when we first seek to trust God with a problem, it will often get worse before it gets better. God does this so that we will see clearly that it is He answering our faith and not just chance. I've seen some amazing answers to prayer attributed to coincidence by young believers who were just learning to crack the faith barrier.

Even Moses got discouraged because of this result and complained to the LORD saying, **"O LORD, why have you brought trouble upon this people? Is this why You sent me? Ever since I went to Pharaoh to speak in Your name, he has brought trouble upon this people, and You have not rescued Your people at all."** (Exodus 5:22-23)

But remember, at the burning-bush encounter the LORD had forewarned Moses that Pharaoh would not let the people go and would harden his heart. But Moses failed to understand what the LORD foretold him, and temporarily lapsed into the human viewpoint.

Moses was about to learn another important facet of combat faith, *to wait on the LORD.* When God delays keeping a promise, it is always for very good reasons, as we will see. But the LORD doesn't always bother to explain those reasons to us. In fact, that is part of the faith-developing process—to teach us to believe Him in situations that are beyond human ability to explain or solve. That's why we have to learn *patience* in believing God. Patience means to believe God in the *long run.* He wants marathon runners, not sprinters, in this race of living by faith.

GOD'S STRONGEST PROMISE

In this time of discouragement, the LORD restated all of the previous covenant promises in the strongest possible terms. He put no conditions on the promises, but declared the emphatic **"I will."** Whenever we see God preface a promise by saying **"I will,"** with no stated conditions, then it is a sovereign commitment on **His** part to perform the promise apart from human merit or performance.

This statement of His promise is very important because it became the basis of why the LORD delivered the Israelites and why He held them accountable to believe Him later. Note carefully what God *unconditionally* promised He would do:

> **God also said to Moses, I am the LORD. I appeared to Abraham, to Isaac and to Jacob as God Almighty, but by My name the LORD [Jehovah] I did not make Myself known to them. I also established My covenant with them TO GIVE THEM the land of Canaan, where they lived as aliens. Moreover, I have heard the groaning of the Israelites, whom the Egyptians are enslaving, and I have remembered My covenant.**
>
> **"Therefore, say to the Israelites: 'I am the LORD, and I *WILL* bring you out from under the yoke of the Egyptians. I *WILL* free you from being slaves to them, and I *WILL* redeem you with an outstretched arm and with mighty acts of judgment. *I WILL* take you as My own people, and *I WILL* be your God. *Then you will know that I am the LORD your God*, who brought you out from under the yoke of the Egyptians. And *I WILL* BRING YOU TO THE LAND I SWORE WITH UPLIFTED HAND [sign of a most solemn oath] TO GIVE TO ABRAHAM, TO ISAAC AND TO JACOB. *I WILL* give it TO YOU as a possession. I Am the LORD.'"** (Exodus 6:2–8)

Moses faithfully declared this great promise to the people both at this time and later. But they didn't listen to him this first time because they were under such increasingly cruel treatment.

Moses was really perplexed by the Israelites' unbelief and increased suffering. So once again, Moses lapsed into the HVP and wavered in his faith. He demonstrated this by what he said when the LORD told him to go to Pharaoh again: *"If the Israelites will not listen to me, why would Pharaoh listen to me, since I speak with faltering lips?"* (6:12) He is clearly analyzing the situation in the light of his ability to deal with it, not God's. At that moment he was not grasping the promises of God *by faith*.

Again the LORD, in beautiful grace, patiently rehearsed to Moses the command and the plan. Once more He told him that He would harden Pharaoh's heart, and that even though He multiplied many miraculous signs and wonders, he would still not listen. The LORD also restated that as a result, He would bring many great judgments on Egypt.

REASONS FOR DELAY

The LORD then revealed several reasons for delaying the Israelites' release and hardening Pharaoh's heart.

The first reason was to evangelize the Egyptians and all the world who would hear of what happened there. Later, just before the plague of hail, Moses, speaking for the LORD, revealed this evangelistic purpose to Pharaoh and his officials: **"But I** [the LORD] **have raised you up for this very purpose, that I might show you my power and that MY NAME MIGHT BE PROCLAIMED IN ALL THE EARTH."** (Exodus 9:16) Many Egyptians did believe in the LORD as a result of witnessing the ten mighty miraculous judgments He brought upon Egypt. Many of the judgments were against idols the Egyptians worshiped, and proved the LORD's superiority over them.

A second reason was to show the Israelites that He indeed was the LORD their God. So God's plan included the evangelization of the Hebrews as well.

A third reason was to allow the Israelites to see firsthand how the LORD literally kept the promises He made to them and their fathers concerning their delivery out of Egypt. In other words they were being given advanced training in the combat faith they would need later.

A fourth reason was to allow time for the news about the many miraculous judgments that broke the power of the world's mightiest nation to spread to the adversaries that Israel would be fighting in the promised land. God was preparing the way for victory, since this news would so terrify them that they would have no heart to fight against Israel's God. As we will see, this was fully accomplished. In fact, one reason God took the Hebrews on the long route to Canaan was so that the news would reach the Canaanites before Israel arrived.

SIGNS AND WONDERS IN JUDGMENT

Moses appeared before Pharaoh and demanded the release of the Israelites eleven more times. The first of these did not result in a judgment, but in a miraculous sign of warning to Pharaoh: Aaron threw his staff down in front of the king and it became a huge snake.

The Occult in Pharaoh's Court

Pharaoh called in his sorcerers, wisemen, and magicians and they duplicated Moses' and Aaron's miracle through **"their secret arts."** But the LORD gave them a warning they should have heeded. The snake from Aaron's staff swallowed all the snakes from the magician's staffs.

It is very important to note that these court occultists duplicated the first three miracles of the LORD through the power of Satan. Satan has the power to work miracles. Therefore, we must be careful to check the source of supernatural phenomena. Too many Christians today automatically assume that any miracle they see must be from the LORD.

In addition to this miracle, the occultists duplicated turning water into blood, and causing frogs to come forth from the dust, just as Moses did through the LORD's power.

But the plague of gnats they could not duplicate and they acknowledged their helplessness to Pharaoh, admitting that, **"This is the finger of God."** (Exodus 8:18-19)

We are warned that in the last days this Satanic duplication of miracles will happen. Jesus predicted, **"For false Christs and false prophets will appear and perform GREAT SIGNS and MIRACLES to deceive even the elect—if that were possible. See, I have told you ahead of time."** (Matthew 24:24-25)

This episode in Pharaoh's court was a prophetic preview

of the kind of deceivers who are coming at the end of the present Church age. The LORD warns about these times: **"But mark this: There will be terrible times in the last days . . . *Just as Jannes and Jambres opposed Moses,* so also these men oppose the truth—men of depraved minds, who, as far as the faith is concerned, are rejected."** (2 Timothy 3:1,8) Jannes and Jambres were the Pharaoh's chief court sorcerers and practitioners of witchcraft. So this is a warning of similar kinds of deceptions. Only the deceptions of the last days will be even worse because these miracle workers will masquerade as ministers of Christ, according to many prophecies.

This brings us to another myth that must be dispelled from Christian thinking: the belief that anyone who does a miracle in the name of Jesus must be genuine. Again, Jesus warned, **"Watch out that no one deceives you. For many will come IN MY NAME, claiming, I am the Christ, and WILL DECEIVE MANY . . . For false Christs and false prophets will appear and perform great signs and miracles TO DECEIVE EVEN THE ELECT—if that were possible."** (Matthew 24:4-5, 24) And Paul warned of a different Jesus: **"For if someone comes to you and preaches a JESUS OTHER THAN THE JESUS we preached, or if you receive a DIFFERENT SPIRIT from the one you received, or a DIFFERENT GOSPEL from the one you accepted, you put up with it easily enough."** (2 Corinthians 11:4) This definitely shows that there is a false Jesus, a false spirit, and a false Gospel, which must be discerned by the doctrine they preach. This is why it is so important to study and *know true doctrine.*

ISRAEL'S GREAT LIBERATION

The miraculous plagues that the LORD wrought through Moses and Aaron virtually destroyed Egypt. To further demonstrate His power and faithfulness to the Israelites, God prevented the plagues from falling on the land of Goshen where the Hebrews lived.

The plagues of turning water to blood, of the millions of frogs, gnats and flies, of killing Egyptian livestock, of boils, of hail, of locusts, of thick darkness, and worst of all, the killing of all the firstborn sons of Egypt, finally broke the will of Pharaoh and his mighty nation.

The last judgment in which all the firstborn sons of Egypt were killed was utterly terrifying. Every home had at least one dead. Because of this the Egyptians urged the Hebrews to leave immediately, even though it was the middle of the night. As the LORD had directed, the Hebrews asked the Egyptians for gold, silver, and clothing, and the people gave it to them gladly to get them out of the land. They feared the LORD would kill them all if the Hebrews stayed a moment longer. This was the LORD's way of collecting the wages owed His people for centuries of slave labor.

But this last judgment had a much greater significance than just finally breaking the back of Egypt, and physically setting the Hebrew people free. . . .

CHAPTER NINE

The Passover:
God's Drama of the Cross

Get rid of the old yeast [leaven] that you may be a
new batch [of dough] without yeast [leaven]—as you
really are. For Christ, our Passover lamb, has been
sacrificed.

1 Corinthians 5:7

The Israelites were not required to do anything to escape the
dreadful supernatural judgments the LORD brought upon
the Egyptians—except for the last one. But when the angel of
the LORD brought death upon all the firstborn of Egypt, the
LORD required each Israelite to do something by faith, or else
come under the same judgment as the Egyptians.

WHEN THE HUMBLE GET ANGRY

There was a pattern to all the previous judgments, with
each judgment becoming progressively worse. Each time the
new plague would fall, Pharaoh would temporarily have a
change of heart and promise to let the Israelites go if Moses
would call off the plague. Then, as soon as it was removed, he
would harden his heart once more.

After Moses prayed away the ninth plague of intense darkness, the following furious dialogue took place:

> But the LORD hardened Pharaoh's heart, and he was not willing to let them go. Pharaoh said to Moses, "Get out of my sight! Make sure you do not appear before me again! The day you see my face you will die."
>
> "Just as you say," MOSES REPLIED, "I will never appear before you again. . . ."
>
> So Moses said, "This is what the LORD says: 'About midnight I will go throughout Egypt. Every firstborn son in Egypt will die, from the firstborn son of Pharaoh, who sits on the throne, to the firstborn son of the slave girl, who is at her hand mill, and all the firstborn of the cattle as well. There will be loud wailing throughout Egypt—worse than there has ever been or ever will be again. But among the Israelites not a dog will bark at any man or animal.' Then you will know that the LORD makes a distinction between Egypt and Israel. All these officials of yours will come to me, bowing down before me and saying, 'Go, you and all the people who follow you!' After that I will leave." Then MOSES, HOT WITH ANGER, left Pharaoh. (Exodus 10:27–29; 11:4–8)

In all the previous appearances before Pharaoh, Moses spoke through Aaron, as the LORD had instructed him. But here the context indicates Moses was so angry with Pharaoh's duplicity, vacillation, and defiance of the LORD, that he spoke directly to the king. I'm sure this was all right with the LORD, for Moses had been talking through Aaron only because he claimed he couldn't speak. Moses' only direct speech to Pharaoh was eloquent.

Humility Is Not Pacifism

Humility and meekness do not assume passivity or the wearing of a sign saying, "Please tread on me." God called

Moses the most humble man on earth, yet He did not rebuke him here for being "hot with anger." There is a time to be righteously angry. Jesus Himself was caught up with "the zeal of His Father's House" when He, in a flame of righteous anger, took the money changers by the seat of their togas and threw them out of the Temple, along with their animals and money-changing tables.

THE NIGHT A NATION WAS SAVED

The LORD, through Moses, gave the Israelites careful instructions, which each one had to keep to the letter by faith. Anyone who didn't believe the LORD would have his home visited by the angel of death.

As many Bible expositors have noted, virtually every aspect of the Passover feast is a prophetic type of the redemptive work of Jesus, the Messiah. The Holy Spirit showed that this symbolism is legitimate when He said,

> **Get rid of the old yeast [leaven] that you may be a new batch without yeast—as you really are. FOR CHRIST, OUR PASSOVER LAMB, has been sacrificed. Therefore let us keep the Festival, not with the old yeast, the yeast of malice and wickedness, but with bread without yeast, the bread of sincerity and truth.** (1 Corinthians 5:7–8)

Paul drew upon the symbolic aspects of the Passover lamb and the preceding seven-day feast of unleavened bread. I'd like to share with you some of my thoughts on the types in the Passover feast, by examining the original feast more closely.

Note the exact instructions the LORD gave each Hebrew family:

> **Then Moses summoned all the elders of Israel and said to them, "Go at once and select the animals for your families and slaughter the Passover lamb. Take a bunch of hyssop [a reed with a spongelike growth on the end], dip it into the blood in the basin and put**

some of the blood on the TOP and on BOTH SIDES of the doorframe." (Exodus 12:21–22)

Now you go stand in a doorway and pretend you are carrying out these instructions. First, raise your arm up to the top of the doorframe, then to one side, then the other side. You just made the sign of the cross. I am sure this is no mere coincidence.

The Israelites were specifically instructed to apply the blood of the lamb **". . . on the doorframes of the house WHERE THEY WOULD EAT THE LAMB."** (Exodus 12:7 HL) The LORD was showing them there was a connection between the blood that saved them and the lamb that sustained them. The LORD Jesus, who saved us through His death, sustains us through His life.

The instructions continue:

> **That same night they are to eat the meat roasted over the fire, along with bitter herbs, and bread made without yeast. Do not eat the meat raw or cooked in water, but roast it over the fire—head, legs and inner parts. Do not leave any of it till morning; if some is left till morning, you must burn it.**
>
> **This is how you are to eat it: with your cloak tucked into your belt, your sandals on your feet and your staff in your hand. Eat it in haste; it is the LORD's Passover.** (Exodus 12:8–11)

There are some beautiful symbols of the person and work of the Messiah here.

The "lamb roasted with fire" is a picture of the righteous judgment of a holy God upon our sins consuming the LORD Jesus in our place. Fire was consistently used in the burnt offerings as a picture of Divine judgment of sin.

The mention of **"the head, legs and inner parts"** could mean this: The **"head"** symbolizes Christ's judgment on behalf of our sinful thoughts, the **"legs"** symbolize our sinful walk, **"the inner parts"** symbolize our old sin nature. All were to be roasted in the fire of God's judgment, so that we might be freed from the penalty and the power of sin. (A similar type of application is made in Leviticus 8:22–30, where blood was applied to Aaron and his sons' right ears, right thumbs, and right big toes. It says that this consecrated them for service before the LORD. The ear was consecrated to hear God's word, the hand was consecrated for God's service, and the foot was consecrated to walk with God.)

It was **"not to be eaten raw,"** which symbolizes that we are not to believe in Christ as just a great moral teacher and religious leader who showed us the way to work our way to God. We must believe in a Christ who was judged (the significance of fire) as a substitute for our sins.

It was **"not to be cooked in water,"** which means we are not to water down the significance of the Messiah's death. He didn't die just as an example of self-sacrifice for His fellow man.

"Eating the lamb" is a particularly precious picture. The same lamb whose blood saves us from judgment and death also sustains, strengthens, and becomes a part of us. This is a picture of the believer meditating upon Christ and by faith being sustained and empowered by His promises and example. It is also a picture of fellowship with the LORD Jesus. When we believe in Him, we enter into a mystical yet actual physical union with Him. We literally become flesh of His flesh and bone of His bone (Ephesians 5:30 NKJV).

The LORD Jesus probably was drawing upon this imagery when he said to the Jews of His day,

> **I tell you the truth, unless you eat the flesh of the Son of Man and drink His blood, you have no life in you.**
>
> **Whoever eats My flesh and drinks My blood has eternal life, and I will raise him up at the last day. . . . Whoever eats My flesh and drinks My blood remains in Me, and I in him. Just as the living Father sent Me and I live because of the Father, so the one who feeds on Me will live because of Me.** (John 6:53–57)

Eating and swallowing is a picture of believing. We must not just chew, but swallow the Gospel so that it too becomes a part of us.

None of the lamb was to be **"left over until morning."** All that was left over was to be burned up with fire. I believe this means that we are not to leave out part of the message of the Gospel, but to believe it all. What we don't believe is lost to us as far as eternal reward is concerned.

The Passover lamb was **"to be eaten with bitter herbs."** This is to remind us of the bitter bondage of sin and the terrible price that was paid for our redemption from it.

For you know that it was not with perishable things such as silver or gold that you were redeemed from the empty way of life handed down to you from your forefathers, but with the precious blood of Christ, a lamb without blemish or defect. (1 Peter 1:18–19)

The lamb was **"to be eaten with the cloak tucked in the belt, with sandals on the feet and the staff in hand."** All of this means that we are to be ready to move out of the place of sin once we are set free from its bondage. Shortly after the Israelites ate the Passover lamb, the LORD's judgment caused the Egyptians to drive them out in the middle of that same night.

What an unforgettable experience that must have been for all the Israelites. They had to believe what God said or die.

On that same night I will pass through Egypt and strike down every firstborn—both men and animals—and I will bring judgment on all the gods of Egypt. I am the LORD. The blood will be a sign for you on the houses where you are; and when I see the blood, I will pass over you. No destructive plague will touch you when I strike Egypt. (Exodus 12:12–13)

Some of the Israelites might have thought to themselves, "This is unreasonable. It just doesn't make sense to me that I should smear that messy blood on my doorframes. And why do I have to stay inside the house?" Nevertheless, everyone who believed God and applied the blood to their doorposts were spared the death of the firstborn—and those who didn't lost the firstborn. But what's more important, all who believed God were justified before God, and His righteousness was credited to their account on the basis of their faith. This was the night in which each Israelite who by faith kept the Passover was given eternal life.

In the same way, a person may not think it reasonable to have to believe in the blood of Christ shed for his sins, but all who do instantly receive eternal life and forgiveness for sin. Anyone who doesn't must ultimately stand before the very One who died for his sins and learn that he is eternally condemned for rejecting a gift of forgiveness for all his other sins. Jesus declared that the Holy Spirit would convict the world of the one unpardonable sin when he said, **"And He, when He comes, will convict the world concerning sin . . . because they do not believe in Me."** (John 16:8–9 NASB)

The Passover was the Israelites' deliverance from the penalty of sin. Crossing the Red sea is a picture of being delivered from the bondage of sin. The Red sea deliverance was an historical illustration of the spiritual deliverance from slavery to the sin nature promised by God in Romans:

> **for sin [nature] shall not be your master, because you are not under law, but under grace . . . But thanks be to God that, though you used to be slaves to sin [nature], you wholeheartedly obeyed the form of teaching to which you were entrusted. You have been set free from sin [nature] and have become slaves to righteousness.** (Romans 6:14,17–18)

The point is that we have been set free from hopeless slavery to Satan and the old sin nature so that we can choose to follow the inner promptings of our new spiritual natures and the indwelling Holy Spirit.

GOD'S PERPETUAL REMINDER TO ISRAEL

The LORD commanded the Israelites never to forget what He did for them that night. This was written to ensure the evangelization of the children of all future generations:

103

Obey these instructions as a lasting ordinance for you and your descendants. When you enter the land that the LORD WILL GIVE YOU AS HE PROMISED, observe this ceremony. And when your children ask you, "What does this ceremony mean to you?" then tell them, "It is the Passover sacrifice to the LORD, who passed over the houses of the Israelites in Egypt and spared our homes when he struck down the Egyptians." Then the people bowed down and worshiped. The Israelites did just what the LORD commanded Moses and Aaron. (Exodus 12:24–28)

If only the people of Israel would heed the meaning behind this feast that they have commemorated for some thirty-four hundred years. It was probably the imagery and teaching of the Passover feast that caused the prophet John the Baptist to exclaim, after he recognized that Jesus was the Messiah, **"Behold, the Lamb of God who takes away the sin of the world."** (John 1:29 NASB)

If you have never seen the LORD Jesus as the One judged in your place under the penalty for your sins, why don't you settle it right now. Just bow your head and say something like this, "LORD Jesus thank You for being my Passover sacrifice. Thank You that what You did is now being applied over the door of my heart so that judgment will not fall on me. Thank You for Your forgiveness. Thank You for eternal life."

If you prayed that prayer, then this promise of the LORD Jesus Christ, who cannot lie, is for you: **"I tell you the truth, whoever hears My word and believes him who sent Me HAS eternal life and will not be condemned; he has crossed over from death to life."** (John 5:24)

CHAPTER TEN

The Battle Is the LORD's

This is what the LORD says to you: "Do not be afraid or discouraged because of this vast army. For the battle is not yours, but God's . . . You will not have to fight this battle."

2 Chronicles 20:15,17

The Scripture tells us the Israelites were in Egypt 430 years to the day when they were released from slavery by the terrified Egyptians (Exodus 12:40–41). And you'll remember they came out with great wealth because the Egyptians gave to them whatever they asked just to hasten their departure.

Listen to what the LORD had predicted to Abraham:

Know for certain that your descendants will be strangers in a country not their own, and they will be enslaved and mistreated four hundred years. But I will punish the nation [Egypt] they serve as slaves, and afterward they will come out with great possessions . . . In the fourth generation your descendants WILL COME BACK HERE . . . (Genesis 15:13–14,16)

(The first thirty years the Israelites were welcome guests because of Joseph's great services to Pharaoh. Afterward, they were made slaves.) This prophecy was exactly fulfilled. Note that in this prophecy the LORD again promised to bring them back to the land of Canaan and give it to them as an everlasting possession. Every Israelite was aware of this promise to Abraham.

THE MIRACLE OF ISRAEL'S FORETOLD HISTORY

This is the first fulfillment of three predicted exiles and restorations of the Hebrew people in history. The other two were the Babylonian dispersion (586 B.C.) and the Roman dispersion (A.D. 70). They began to return from the Babylonian exile in 516 B.C., and from the worldwide exile induced by the Roman holocaust to officially become a nation on A.D. May 14, 1948.

Israel's major history has all been exactly predicted and precisely fulfilled. Any skeptic who treats these facts fairly must conclude that the Bible is God's inspired Word. No mere men could have made such accurate predictions over a period of so many centuries and have had them all exactly fulfilled.

THE POPULATION OF THE EXODUS

When Joseph brought his father Jacob, his brothers, and their families into Egypt to escape the famine that was in Canaan, they numbered about seventy persons. Just before Jacob left Canaan the LORD appeared to him and promised,

> **Jacob! Jacob! . . . I am God, the God of your father. Do not be afraid to go down to Egypt, for I will make you into a great nation there. I will go down to Egypt with you, and I WILL SURELY BRING YOU BACK AGAIN.** (Genesis 46:3-4)

The night Israel was set free, the Scripture says, **"There were about six hundred thousand men on foot, besides women and children. Many other people went up with them** [These were Egyptians and other refugees who had believed in the God of Israel], **as well as large droves of livestock both flocks and herds."** (Exodus 12:37-38)

A conservative estimate of the total population, counting one wife and only three children to each adult man, would equal 3,000,000. When the non-Israelites are added it would be in excess of 3,000,000. Add at least 1,500,000 head of livestock, and we begin to get a picture of the enormously complicated logistics of the Exodus. How would you like to be responsible for supplying food and water for such a group? God's prediction that He would make the Hebrews into a mighty nation in Egypt was fulfilled to the letter.

Another important prophecy was fulfilled that night. Remember Joseph's unburied coffin, which had been a witness that the LORD would rescue the Hebrews and return them to the land of Canaan? The Scripture says, **"Moses took the bones of Joseph with him because Joseph had made the sons of Israel swear an oath. He had said, 'God will surely come to your aid, and then you must carry my bones up with you from this place.'"** (Exodus 13:20)

All of this adds up to one imperative lesson: *God Keeps His Promises!* This is the foundation for cracking the faith barrier and entering the realm of combat faith.

THE LORD'S STRANGE LEADING

As the people prepared to leave Egypt, the LORD gathered them together in Rameses, which was in the northeast sector of Egypt in the province of Goshen. They were organized into marching order by tribes. Just as they were about to move out, an awesome phenomenon took place. The LORD came down in a pillar of fire and stood before the assembled ranks. This was the beginning of a procedure that lasted as long as Israel was in the wilderness. The LORD led them by night in a pillar of fire, and by day in a pillar of cloud. This gave them light by night, and by day, in the blazing heat of the Sinai desert, God provided them with shade. When the pillar stopped, they knew they were to camp. When it moved, they knew they were to follow. (Exodus 13:21–22) No people have ever had more definite guidance concerning where God wanted them to be, wouldn't you agree?

The LORD led the people about ninety miles southeast

from Rameses to Succoth, which was on the main caravan route to Canaan. Then He turned them eastward on that route to a place on the edge of the desert called Etham, where they camped. (Exodus 12:37; 13:20) So far, so good! Everything appeared to be logical and normal. They were on the "super highway" to Canaan. I'm sure the Israelites expected to be in the promised land within a couple of weeks.

WHERE'S THAT PILLAR GOING NOW?

But then the strangest thing happened. The LORD, in His pillar of cloud, turned back to the north instead of to the east. He began to lead them back into the general direction from which they, with considerable effort, had just come. I'm sure the Israelites began to murmur, "Hey, this isn't the way to Canaan. Why are we going north? It's hard to move all these people and animals, so why are we returning to the area from which we just came? There are no routes to Canaan up there. In fact there is only the sea."

THE LORD'S WAY OF LEADING

The LORD said to Moses, **"Tell the Israelites to turn back and encamp near Pi Hahiroth, between Migdol and the sea. They are to encamp by the sea, directly opposite Baal Zephon."** (Exodus 14:2)

Now look at the map of the Exodus on page 111. The LORD told them to camp at a place where they had the sea to their north and east. To make it even more confusing, there were no possible passageways from that location to their destination of Canaan. From a military point of view, it made even less sense. It was the most dangerous possible place to be camped if Pharaoh changed his mind (which he had done on all previous occasions), and decided to attack them with his still mighty army.

Yet, this was without doubt the place to which the LORD had led them. Why in the world did God do such a "crazy" thing? There is a very important principle to be seen here.

Sometimes God's leading for our life doesn't make sense at all from the human viewpoint. But if we just keep trusting Him, He will ultimately bless us, and teach us how to crack the faith barrier in the process.

PHARAOH TAKES THE BAIT

The LORD explained some of the reasoning behind His strange plan:

Then the LORD said to Moses, ". . . Pharaoh will think, 'The Israelites are wandering around the land in confusion, HEMMED IN BY THE DESERT.' And I will harden Pharaoh's heart, and he will pursue them. But I will gain glory for myself through Pharaoh and all his army, and the Egyptians will know that I am the LORD." (Exodus 14:3-4)

The LORD did not tell Moses *how* he would get glory over Pharaoh and his army. But the LORD did say that the Egyptian people would be brought to know He is superior to all man-made gods.

Pharaoh did exactly what the LORD said he would do. Thinking that the Israelites were confused and moving around in circles, he quickly mobilized his army. He selected six hundred of his best charioteers to lead the other chariots. (A chariot in that day would be equivalent to a battle tank today. People on foot were almost defenseless against them.)

He mobilized his cavalry, as well as his vast, highly trained infantry. This was the finest and best-equipped army in the world. From the human viewpoint, the Israelites didn't stand a chance. Pharaoh and the Egyptians believed there would be an easy revenge for all the death and destruction the Hebrews had brought upon them.

ISRAEL'S GLORIOUS OPPORTUNITY—FUMBLED!

The Holy Spirit describes the fearful scene:

The Egyptians—all Pharaoh's horses and chariots, horsemen and troops—pursued the Israelites and overtook them as they camped by the sea near Pi Hahiroth, opposite Baal Zephon. As Pharaoh approached, the Israelites LOOKED UP, and there were the Egyptians, marching after them. (Exodus 14:9–10a)

The critical test had come. Remember what these people had witnessed: without an army, without human help, the LORD had made the mightiest military power of that time set the Hebrew slaves free; the Hebrews all had heard the LORD's promises to deliver them from Pharaoh and Egypt, to take them to the land of Canaan, and to give it to them as an everlasting possession; they had all seen with their own eyes the unprecedented and awesome ten miraculous judgments the LORD brought upon Egypt. Now God expected them to apply all this evidence of His veracity and faithfulness to the current impossible situation.

But alas, there was no such response. When the Israelites **"looked up"** and saw the chariots approaching, THEY DIDN'T LOOK HIGH ENOUGH. Instead of seeing the LORD, they saw only the terrifying sight of Pharaoh's crack troops rapidly closing in on them, cutting off all avenues of escape. They saw the flashing blades on the hubs of the chariot wheels that would cut people down like a lawnmower does tall grass. They saw the soldiers in endless rows, spears and swords flashing, as they charged toward them.

Men panicked, women screamed, children ran, animals stampeded. The camp was a chaos of terrified, unbelieving people.

But in all this, one thing was clear—the LORD had *deliberately* led them into this hopeless predicament. "Why us, LORD?" they must have screamed as they proceeded to fall apart. But before we judge them too harshly, suppose you had been there? It is well and good to talk about trusting God's promises when you are not in a life-threatening crisis. But if you had been there, would *you* have gone by what your eyes saw, or believed what God had promised?

The Israelites knew what the LORD had done for them in

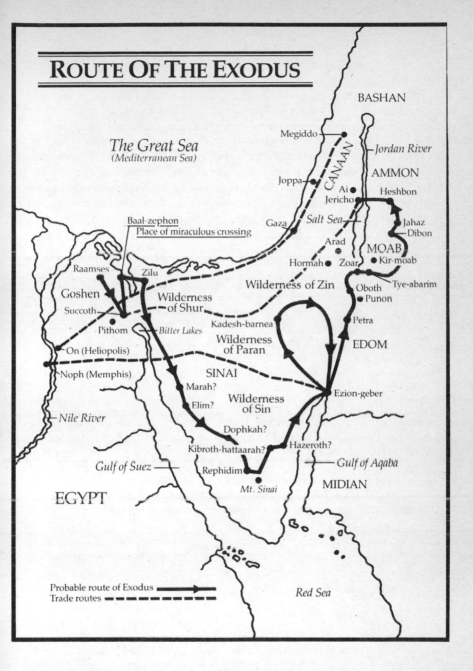

ROUTE OF THE EXODUS

BASHAN

The Great Sea
(Mediterranean Sea)

Megiddo

CANAAN

Jordan River

AMMON

Joppa

Ai
Jericho

Heshbon

Baal-zephon
Place of miraculous crossing

Gaza

Salt Sea

Jahaz
Dibon

Raamses

Zilu

Arad

MOAB

Goshen

Wilderness
of Shur

Hormah

Zoar

Kir-moab

Succoth

Wilderness of Zin

Oboth

Tye-abarim

Pithom

Bitter Lakes

Kadesh-barnea

Punon

On (Heliopolis)

Wilderness
of Paran

Petra

Noph (Memphis)

SINAI

EDOM

Marah?

Ezion-geber

Nile River

Elim?

Wilderness
of Sin

Dophkah?

Kibroth-hattaarah?

Hazeroth?

Gulf of Aqaba

Gulf of Suez

Rephidim

MIDIAN

EGYPT

Mt. Sinai

Probable route of Exodus
Trade routes

Red Sea

the past. They knew what the LORD had promised about their future. But why was the LORD making things so difficult? The answer to that is the very essence of this book's message. You see, the only way we can learn to crack the faith barrier is to believe God in the midst of unexplained, impossible situations, when circumstances seem to be going against all that God has promised, and the only hope we have is to cling tenaciously to those very promises. It's remembering that in every circumstance, no matter how grim, God's ultimate purpose is to bless us, if we only keep trusting Him. God doesn't allow trials into our lives to make us miserable. When we boldly claim His promises, He delivers us!

"SPIRITUAL GEOMETRY?"

Now what *did* the LORD expect of these children of His? He expected them to apply what I call "spiritual geometry." That is, if you know the measurements of any two sides of a right triangle, you can figure out the measurements of the unknown side. They knew the base of God's triangle—they had been released from bondage to Pharaoh by many miraculous signs. They knew the height of the triangle—they had God's oft-repeated solemn promise to take them to Canaan and give it to them. Now they have situation "X"—the unknown hypotenuse of the triangle. All they had to do was add A^2 and B^2 to get C^2 or "X." In other words, God expected them to add together their previous experiences of seeing His faithfulness and come up with the only possible answer: God must be planning some extraordinary action to deliver them!

They should have said: *"LORD, what a glorious opportunity to trust you! We can't wait to see what you are going to do with this Egyptian army! You told us that You are taking us to the promised land, and this army is in the way. You led us here, now deal with them by the same power You used to get us this far."*

But instead, just listen to what the Israelites said:

They were terrified and cried out to the LORD. They said to Moses, "Was it because there were no graves

in Egypt that you brought us to the desert to die? What have you done to us by bringing us out of Egypt? Didn't we say to you in Egypt, 'Leave us alone; let us serve the Egyptians'? It would have been better for us to serve the Egyptians than to die in the desert!" (Exodus 14:10b–12)

Now that's gratitude, isn't it? When people switch to the human viewpoint, they start griping about their circumstances and refuse to recognize that God sets up the circumstances. They tend to blame their situation on everyone else. It's especially easy to blame the nearest leader. Poor Moses. All he did was act as God's instrument to deliver their miserable hides from bondage, and now they get angry with him for setting them free.

MOSES CRACKS THE FAITH BARRIER

Into the midst of this chaos Moses shouted,

"Do not be afraid. STAND STILL, and see the salvation of the LORD, which He will accomplish for you today. For the Egyptians whom you see today, you shall see again no more forever. The LORD WILL FIGHT FOR YOU, and you shall hold your peace." (Exodus 14:13 NKJV)

This is one of the greatest single acts of faith recorded in the Bible. Moses did not have any more to go on than any of the other Israelites who were by now in total hysteria.

Moses refused to go by his emotions. He refused to let what his five senses were telling him overrule what God had sworn to do. Remember the pilot who flew into the clouds and believed his senses instead of the flight instruments? Unlike him, Moses flew by God's spiritual flight instruments—His promises.

Moses truly saw the situation from the Divine viewpoint. He knew that no amount of military genius, organization, or weapons could save the Israelites from the oncoming Egyptian army. **He added up all the facts, and his faith concluded that God Himself had to destroy the Egyptian army, for His name was at stake.** So Moses cracked the faith barrier and entered a spiritual dimension where there is inner peace and confidence in spite of impossible odds and fearful circumstances, a dimension where the eye of faith sees God in complete control.

WHEN IT'S WRONG TO PRAY

After Moses made this incredible statement of faith, he did a totally surprising thing. You see, at this point, Moses still didn't know **how** God was going to deliver Israel. We are told, **"Then the LORD said to Moses, 'Why are you crying out to Me?'"** (Exodus 14:15a)

Right after his great statement of faith, Moses had cried out to God in prayer and probably said something like, "Okay, LORD, I've believed you—now do something! Those Egyptian chariots are closing in fast. I don't know what you are going to do, LORD, but You had better get started right away!"

Next God said to Moses,

Tell the sons of Israel to go forward [toward the sea]. **And as for you, LIFT UP YOUR STAFF AND STRETCH OUT YOUR HAND OVER THE SEA AND DIVIDE IT, and the sons of Israel shall go through the midst of the sea on dry land.** (Exodus 14:15b–16 NASB)

The LORD in essence told Moses, "Look, you have already believed My promises, and you know what My will is. If you cry out to Me now, it is unbelief. You march out there and stand on the authority of My word, lift up your rod and divide the sea. You are going by faith, not by your feelings; you are filled with combat faith. So get up and move forward!"

There is a time to pray, and there is a time to simply believe that what you have prayed has already been granted and to act upon it. It was at this point that Moses moved into the experience of **combat faith.** Don't leave home without it!

HOW ONE MAN'S FAITH SAVED A NATION

As far as we know, no one but Moses had combat faith that day. His faith alone was the basis upon which God was set free to act—and oh, how He did act! The first thing the LORD did was to put a screen of protection between Pharaoh's hard-charging army and the Israelites:

> **Then the angel of God, who had been traveling in front of Israel's army, withdrew and went behind them. The pillar of cloud also moved from in front and stood behind them, coming between the armies of Egypt and Israel. Throughout the night the cloud brought darkness to the one side and light to the other side; so neither went near the other all night long.** (Exodus 14:19–20)

The Angel of the LORD in the Old Testament is the member of the Godhead who became incarnate in the LORD Jesus, the Messiah. Just think of it, the pre-incarnate Christ was there, holding off the army of Egypt so that Moses would have time to call forth a mighty delivering miracle of God. This is why the LORD Jesus said to the rabbis of His day, **"If you believed Moses, you would believe Me, for he wrote about Me."** (John 5:46)

While the angel of the LORD, with His pillar of cloud, held off the army, Moses exercised combat faith:

> **Then Moses stretched out his hand over the sea, and all that night the LORD drove the sea back with a strong east wind and turned it into DRY LAND. The waters were divided, and the Israelites went through the sea on DRY GROUND, with a wall of water on their right and on their left.** (Exodus 14:21–22)

THE BAPTISM OF MOSES

This was such a miracle of Moses' faith alone that the Holy Spirit says all who walked through the sea with Moses that

115

day were "baptized into Moses." (1 Corinthians 10:1–2) Now this is a perfect illustration of the metaphorical sense in which the original Greek word *baptizo* is used in the New Testament. Who got wet that day? The Israelites certainly didn't. It clearly says, "the Israelites went through the sea on dry ground." It was the Egyptians who got wet, yet they were not baptized.

Baptizo is used metaphorically to mean that those who by faith followed Moses were totally *identified* with him and his faith, so that their destinies were changed. Instead of staying and being put to death, they followed the faith act of one man, Moses, and lived.

This is a wonderful parallel with our Savior, who through His one act of obedience and death in our place opened the path to eternal life for all who will believe in Him (See Romans 5:12–19). The instant we believe in what Jesus the Messiah did for us, we are baptized by the Holy Spirit into an eternal, personal union with Him. We are completely identified with Him and become a member of His body, His flesh, and His bone (Ephesians 5:30 KJV). His righteousness becomes our righteousness. His life, which is eternal, becomes our life. His inheritance becomes our inheritance. His destiny becomes our destiny. All of this is because of our union with Him, which is expressed in the Epistles by the phrase, **in Christ.**

This union with Christ is the ground of our awesome authority, which God has granted to every believer today. Most believers don't ever learn about this authority, much less exercise it. But it is available to all who will claim it by faith. On this point, the Scripture says,

> **But because of His great love for us, God, who is rich in mercy, made us alive with Christ even when we were dead in transgressions—it is by grace you have been saved. And God raised us up with Christ and SEATED US WITH HIM in the heavenly realms IN CHRIST JESUS.** (Ephesians 2:4–6)

We are seated with Christ on His throne through our union with Him and share the authority of His throne. This gives us the same kind of authority to release God's power as Moses had, as long as it is used to accomplish God's will. All God's promises, of course, assume that the one claiming them knows God's will and is seeking His glory and not his own.

MOSES' REPUTATION: FROM HERO TO BUM TO HERO

After Israel was safely on its way across the sea, the LORD moved the dark side of the pillar of cloud behind them. Pharaoh and his army arose and insanely pursued Israel through the divided sea. When they drew too close to the Israelites, the angel of God threw them into confusion: He bogged down the chariot wheels and made them swerve, spooked the horses, and frightened the soldiers. The Egyptians were terrified and said, **"Let's get away from the Israelites! The LORD is fighting for them against Egypt!"**

The Scripture tells us the outcome:

> Then the LORD said to Moses, "Stretch out your hand over the sea so that the waters may flow back over the Egyptians and their chariots and horsemen." Moses stretched out his hand over the sea, and at daybreak the sea went back to its place. The Egyptians were fleeing toward it, and the LORD swept them into the sea. The water flowed back and covered the chariots and horsemen—the entire army of Pharaoh that had followed the Israelites into the sea. Not one of them survived.
>
> But the Israelites went through the sea on dry ground, with a wall of water on their right and on their left. That day the LORD saved Israel from the hands of the Egyptians, and Israel saw the Egyptians lying dead on the shore. And when the Israelites saw the great power the LORD displayed against the Egyptians, the people feared the LORD and put their trust in Him and IN MOSES His servant. (Exodus 14:25–31)

So after the LORD saved the Israelites by Moses' faith, they honored him again as they had when the great miraculous judgments of God had forced Pharaoh to let them go. At least for the moment, Moses was not the bum who had led them out into the desert to be massacred.

117

ISRAEL'S 20/20 HINDSIGHT FAITH

The Israelites were badly infected with faith-after-the-fact-itis. They displayed signs of this illness throughout the rest of the Exodus. The people trusted the LORD and His servant, Moses, all the way—till the next test, which was not long in coming.

THE RED SEA AND YOU

The deliverance at the Red sea has a tremendous application to our lives today. Though the LORD may allow us to be led into a similar impossible situation, His will is that we boldly stand against the odds and claim His promises. When we do, He delivers us.

There have been times when I have traveled to distant places to minister and have been struck down by sickness. I knew in these cases that the LORD had not brought me there to lie in bed, so I rebuked the sickness in the name of Jesus and it left. I got up and proclaimed the Gospel with renewed power, because the very incident increased my faith, which was the purpose of the test in the first place.

There was a time when an atheistic professor was seeking to ban all Christian activity on the college campus. The Christian students prayed and claimed promises that God would remove the hindrance. To our surprise, the LORD removed the obstacle by causing the professor to drop dead shortly thereafter. All the believers moved with an awakened awe of God's power and holiness afterward.

In most cases, as soon as we react to a trial with faith in the LORD's promises, He removes it. If He doesn't, then we know that there is some greater lesson He desires to teach us concerning perseverance in faith.

Always remember that though God's leading may be unexplainable for the moment, His ultimate purpose is to teach us to believe Him so that we may have inner peace, joy, and effective service for Him now, and great rewards in eternity.

CHAPTER ELEVEN

Snatching Defeat from the Jaws of Victory

When our fathers were in Egypt,
they gave no thought to Your miracles;
    they did not remember Your
    many kindnesses,
and they rebelled by the sea, the Red
    Sea.
Yet [He] saved them for [His] name's
    sake . . .

                      Psalms 106:7–8

THE CURSE OF A SHORT MEMORY

Israel sang a beautiful song of praise to the LORD after the great deliverance from the Egyptians. In fact this hymn of praise had some tremendous insights about the LORD and the impact the news of the destruction of the Egyptian army would have upon the inhabitants of the promised land, whom the Israelites would soon have to fight.

Listen to the words they sang:

The nations will hear and tremble;
anguish will grip the people of PHILISTIA.

119

**The chiefs of EDOM will be terrified,
the leaders of MOAB will be seized with trembling,
the people of CANAAN will melt away;
terror and dread will fall upon them. . . .**
    (Exodus 15:14–16)

This song was truly prophetic. Rahab of Jericho reveals how all of the inhabitants of the promised land were paralyzed with fear when they heard of how the LORD of Israel fought for them against the Egyptians and other countries en route (see Joshua 2:8–11).

If only the Israelites would have remembered this song of faith when they arrived at the borders of their adversaries. One of the most common problems these believers had, when it came to trusting God, was a short memory. But then, we can understand that, can't we? We also sing in church about the faithfulness and power of the LORD and promptly forget them when trials come. Remember the personal prayer logs I spoke about in chapter four? Those records remind us of the incredible things that God has done to supply our every need in the past so we're not so tempted to doubt Him in the present, and are a tremendous source of encouragement when under trials.

THE "WRONG KIND OF WATER" TEST

After a night of dancing and rejoicing, the LORD led the Israelites by His pillar of cloud out into the desert. For three days they found no water. Finally they arrived at an oasis with a large pool. But when they took a drink, they found, to their horror, that the water was bitter and undrinkable.

This was no small problem. Remember, there were in excess of three million thirsty people, and about a million and a half equally thirsty animals.

Now why do you think the LORD *again* deliberately led them into this situation? (And it was certain that the LORD had led them there.) It should have been clear by now that He cared what happened to them. And it should have been equally apparent that the LORD had the power to take care of the details involved in keeping His promise to take them to Canaan.

So how did the people respond to this situation?

> **When they came to Marah [meaning "bitter"], they could not drink its water because it was bitter. (That is why the place is called Marah.) So the people GRUMBLED against Moses, saying, "What are we to drink?"**
>
> **Then Moses cried out to the LORD, and the LORD showed him a tree. He threw it into the water, and the water became sweet.** (Exodus 15:23–25)

ONE OF LIFE'S MOST DANGEROUS ADDICTIONS—GRUMBLING

The Israelites had discovered a new pastime, namely, grumbling against Moses. Their motto from here on out seems to have been, "When in doubt, grumble at Moses!" But grumbling or griping about life's circumstances is an extremely dangerous habit because it soon becomes an addiction.

When a child of God doesn't want to trust the LORD, he rarely has the guts to blame Him directly for his adversity. It's always safer to somehow divorce the circumstances from the LORD and blame them on "fate" or some other human being. But it is impossible to separate our circumstances from the LORD, because nothing happens in our lives apart from His will. And if God permits a trial in our lives, it's because He intends to ultimately work it together for our good.

What did the LORD expect of the Israelites in this situation? Instead of grumbling, the LORD expected these people to say something like, "LORD, we failed to trust you at the Red sea. But after seeing your power and faithfulness, we have learned our lesson. We know You didn't lead us out here to kill us, so we will just claim Your promise and praise You until You fix the water."

But alas, no such response was forthcoming. They failed

to understand the principle that nothing comes into a child of God's life without the LORD's permission. This is especially true when the believer knows he is in God's will. The Israelites refused to see that complaining about the circumstances of life was in reality complaining against God, Who always filters our circumstances with a view toward His ultimate purpose of blessing. Grumbling at God is a very serious matter indeed.

Human nature has not changed. We still do exactly the same thing today. There is no way to begin trusting the LORD until we accept the fact that nothing touches us unless He allows it. This is why I must now repeat one of the most important promises in the Bible: **"And we know that God causes all things to work together for good to those who love God, to those who are called according to His purpose."** (Romans 8:28 NASB) This promise does not say that all things are good, but rather that God will work them together for good. God can even work our sin together for good when we repent and believe Him.

GROWING FROM SMALLER TO GREATER FAITH EXPLOITS

It wasn't good that the Israelites had run out of water. Nor was it good that the only water available was bitter and impossible to drink. But the LORD had obviously set up this situation in order to prepare them for the greater challenges to come. In this way the LORD was preparing them for the bigger trials of combat in the conquest of the promised land. The lesson for us is clear—if we don't learn to trust God's promises in the little, everyday things, we will certainly not believe Him when a real crisis comes along. If we develop a pattern of unbelief, we are in for a miserable life.

God shows us a definite spiritual principle by the experiences of the Exodus generation: As we respond to tests of our faith in the present, so we will likely respond to them in the future. Each one of us is daily developing either a pattern of belief or unbelief. There just isn't any neutral ground on this issue.

122

THE DYNAMICS OF PRAISE

However, when we believe the truth of Romans 8:28, then we are able to express our faith in the way most pleasing to God. The LORD reveals how important praise is to Him in this verse: **"In everything give thanks; for this** [whatever is happening in your life] **is God's will for you in Christ Jesus."** (1 Thessalonians 5:18 NASB)

The greatest way to express our faith is to praise the LORD in our trials. On the other hand, the supreme way to express our unbelief is to grumble and complain about our circumstances. This is why the LORD took Israel's grumbling so seriously and rated it as evidence of its greatest sin—unbelief!

But how can you thank the LORD, when you've just lost your job, or when your best friend betrays you, or when your husband comes in and says that he is leaving you, or when someone you love dies? There is only one way. You must believe that in spite of your pain and agony, God, in His overall plan, will ultimately work it together for good if you trust Him. God holds Job up as the supreme example of this kind of faith-praise. This is how Job responded to the news that all of his children had been killed and his wealth destroyed:

**"Naked I came from my mother's womb,
and naked I will depart.
The LORD gave and the LORD has taken away;
may the name of the LORD be praised.**

In all this, Job DID NOT SIN by charging God with wrongdoing." (Job 1:21–22)

(A popular television Bible teacher has said that Job was in error when he said, **"the LORD has taken away."** It's so important to look at the context of every passage. In this case, God commended Job for such a statement of faith by saying, **"In all this, Job DID NOT SIN by charging God with wrongdoing."** We can't say the same for this TV teacher, however, for his statement charged God's Word with error. Poor Job is really getting a working over from several other well-known TV teachers, because he just blows out of the water their dogmatic assertions that it's God's will for all Christians to be continually prosperous and free from trials. But over and against this false teaching, God's Word commends Job as one of the greatest examples of faith in the Bible.) (See also Ezekiel 14:14, 20, and James 5:11 concerning God's estimation of Job.)

FAITH IS LIKE A MUSCLE

I was taught in my early days as a new believer that in many ways faith is like a muscle. A muscle has to be stretched to its limit of endurance in order to build more strength. If we don't increase stress in training, muscle will not grow. In the same way faith must be tested to the limit of its endurance in order to expand and develop.

There is no standing still in the spiritual growth process. A believer is either progressing or regressing in his maturity at any given time. No status quo exists here. Still it takes time to develop a strong and enduring faith. Most of us can no more trust God for big things at the beginning of our faith training than we can go out and run a marathon without training.

GOD'S SOLUTION FOR BITTERNESS—A TREE

Back at Marah, the LORD showed Moses a tree and told him to throw it into the water. As soon as he did, it became sweet. How gracious the LORD is. He didn't even rebuke the people for their unbelief and grumblings against Him. He gave them every chance to grow. In pure grace, the LORD gave them sweet water to drink.

This wasn't the only time that God would take the bitterness out of life by using a tree. I believe that this was a type of the cross. When we apply the significance of the tree on which the LORD Jesus died to the bitterness of our life, He transforms our situation into something sweet and refreshing.

THE LORD WHO HEALS

When the LORD healed the bitter water, He gave the Israelites a great promise:

124

There the LORD made a decree and a law for them, and there He TESTED them. He said, "If you listen carefully to the voice of the LORD your God and do what is right in His eyes, if you pay attention to His commands and keep all His decrees, I will not bring on you any of the DISEASES I brought on the Egyptians, for I AM THE LORD, WHO HEALS YOU." (Exodus 15:25b–26)

This is one of those amazing and wonderful promises that the LORD gave to Israel. Diseases of all kinds were rampant in Egypt, as they were in the rest of the ancient world. This was mainly because of the unsanitary way food was handled and prepared, and the fact that people didn't wash their hands before eating or appreciate the importance of placing diseased persons and animals under quarantine.

The LORD gave Israel intricate laws concerning which foods to eat, food sanitation, food preparation, personal hygiene, quarantine, and so on. In the light of today's medical knowledge, the dietary and sanitation commandments of the Law of Moses are even more of a marvel. Thousands of years before doctors discovered that diseases are transmitted via germs and bacteria, the LORD gave certain ordinances to protect Israel from them.

This is one of the reasons the LORD made escaping the diseases of Egypt contingent on keeping His commandments. It was partly because of the dietary-sanitation section of the Law of Moses that Israel was the healthiest nation in the ancient world. The Israelites also had the most perfect nutritionally balanced food of all time while they were in the desert. God Himself prepared this food called *manna*.

The Scripture quoted above is also a gracious promise of supernatural healing. I believe that we can claim this promise today as we pray over the sick and expect the LORD to heal them in accordance with His will. If you have claimed God's promise for healing, and the LORD's answer to you is "Wait," you can rest assured He has a very special purpose, plan, and reward for your patience. But there has been a dramatic increase in the healing ministry of the Holy Spirit in these last days due to a resurgence of faith in what God promised to do all through the Church age.

PALM SPRINGS OF SINAI

After the desperate Israelites were tested at the bitter (actually poison) waters of Marah, they arrived at Elim. The Bible says, **"Then they came to Elim, where there were twelve springs and seventy palm trees, and they camped there near the water."** (Exodus 15:27)

Elim (which means "trees") was no more than ten miles from Marah. In the Sinai, twelve springs of artesian water with seventy date palms is a paradise indeed.

It is important to note that the LORD first led the people directly to the place where they would have to trust Him to heal the water, before bringing them here to this gorgeous oasis. The LORD, who knows all things, could have bypassed Marah and brought them directly to Elim, couldn't He? But as we have repeatedly seen, when the LORD deems it necessary, He leads His children directly into tests, so that their faith will grow.

This passage gives us another wonderful spiritual principle: After the tests of Marah there is always the joy of Elim just up the road. The psalmist put the principle this way: **"For His anger lasts only a moment, but His favor lasts a lifetime; weeping may remain for a night, but rejoicing comes in the morning."** (Psalm 30:5)

The real lesson behind all the case histories we have examined is that in all our experiences, whether in good times or hard times, the LORD wants us to learn the secret shared by the Apostle Paul:

> **I am not saying this because I am in need, for I have learned to be content whatever the circumstances. I know what it is to be in need, and I know what it is to have plenty. I have learned the secret of BEING CONTENT in any and every situation, whether well fed or hungry, whether living in plenty or in want. I can do everything through Him who gives me strength.** (Philippians 4:11–13)

CHAPTER TWELVE

The No Food,
No Water Test

"Man does not live on bread alone, but on every
word that comes from the mouth of God."
Matthew 4:4

The Israelites apparently enjoyed the lush oasis of Elim, so the
LORD let them stay there over a month. I say this because it
took the Israelites three days to arrive at Marah and Elim. The
Bible says they left Elim on the fifteenth day of the second
month after leaving Egypt. This means that they stayed at Elim
about forty-two days. This small detail simply shows that the
LORD cares about the little needs of His children, as well as
the big ones. He gave them time to get oriented to the new
nomadic desert life, and to rest and recuperate from the emo-
tional strain of the previous tests.

But as soon as they left the relative comfort and security of
Elim and entered the Desert of Sin (a Hebrew name for the
desert between Elim and Sinai, which doesn't have the meaning of the English word *sin*), trouble started. The Desert of Sin
extends southward from Elim to the region of Mount Sinai
(Exodus 16:1). Check the map of the Exodus. This is a wild,
barren, and difficult land, with very few fresh-water sources.

Moses had to be living by combat faith just to lead all

those people and animals out into this area. Even if there had been modern supermarkets along the way, there still wouldn't have been enough food to supply three million people and their animals. But the LORD's pillar of cloud moved forth and Moses, resting by faith in His promises, rallied the people and plunged in after Him.

SURPRISE! SURPRISE! . . . ISRAEL GRIPES AGAIN!

As they moved farther into the wilderness, the Bible says,

In the desert the whole community GRUMBLED against Moses and Aaron. The Israelites said to them, "If only we had died by the LORD's hand in Egypt! There we sat around pots of meat and ate all the food we wanted, but you have brought us out into this desert to starve this entire assembly to death." (Exodus 16:2-3)

Can you believe that? After all the LORD had done in their sight, and while He was visibly leading them, they came up with this incredible statement of unbelief.

Notice their selective memory as they looked back to Egypt. Somehow, all they could remember was the food! They conveniently forgot four hundred years of horrible slavery, suffering, and hopelessness. They proceeded to accuse their liberators, poor old Moses and Aaron, of trying to kill them!

Finally, they refused once again to see the connection between their circumstances and the LORD's direct leading, proven faithfulness, and unconditional promises. So back they went to their standard operating procedure, "When in doubt, grumble at Moses!"

THE SIN OF LOOKING BACK

We Christians often do the same sort of thing that these Israelites did. When we get out of fellowship, it's easy to look back to "the good old days" before we were saved. Also, when the LORD allows a trial into our life for the purpose of teaching us faith, we can fall into the trap of feeling sorry for ourselves and selectively remembering some of the "good times" of the old life. Of course the Devil helps us conveniently forget the misery, despair, and emptiness that ultimately comes from a life that is separated from God. As the Bible says, sin can be pleasurable for a season. But it always exacts a heavy toll in the end.

Satan can make the "good old days" ever so attractive, especially when we are being trained to crack the faith barrier through various tests. Satan has the power to put on a dazzling display of temptation at just the moment when our faith is staggering and we are feeling sorry for ourselves.

Remember that Satan, while tempting Jesus to bypass the cross and worship him, showed Him "**. . . in an instant all the kingdoms of the world. And he said to Him, 'I will give you all their authority and splendor, for it has been given to me, and I can give it to anyone I want to.'**" (Luke 4:5-6) Satan wasn't making idle boasts. He had the title deed to the world and could give it to whomever he pleased. But the important thing is that he had the power to show the world kingdoms in all their glory and splendor and to conceal all the heartache and misery in them caused by sin.

In only a month and a half, Satan blinded the Israelites to their four hundred years of misery and captivity. You may find this incredible, but today we have even less excuse for not trusting God than the Israelites did. We have the completed record of God's faithfulness to His people in the Bible. We've inherited more than seven thousand promises in Scripture, which cover every possible area of need we could have in this life.

THE WORST SIN CHRISTIANS COMMIT

Underlying the Israelites' continuing failure in the Exodus was a glaring manifestation of their inner disbelief—*worrying*! Their worry was shown by their constant griping and expressions of panic and fear. Actually, the worst sin a Christian can commit is to worry. You cannot worry and believe God's promises at the same time. Worry is the maximum expression of a lack of faith in the LORD's faithfulness and love for you.

When we worry, we are in effect saying to God, "You don't care about me and my needs, and You don't really mean what You promised! Oh sure, You died for my sins, but You don't care enough to provide for me in my daily life."

Worry is socially acceptable in the Church today. After all, everybody worries, right? When was the last time you witnessed something like this in your church: "The pastor and elders have decided to excommunicate brother Charles from our fellowship for the gross sin of 'worrying.' He will be barred from our congregation until he repents of this wickedness." I'm sure that such an issue has never been made in your remembrance. Yet the Bible makes it clear that worry is one of the worst sins that we can commit against the LORD personally. We should judge this sin with the same seriousness as we would murder, theft, and the more common sins.

Here are two common examples of the situations in which we worry instead of believing the LORD's promises:

When you get sick and you are hit with a massive unexpected hospital bill, do you start worrying, or do you trust the LORD and rest in His promise to supply your needs?

When you've been walking with the LORD, and the company for which you've worked the last twenty years lays you off, do you become bitter and anxious and curse your circumstances, or do you trust the LORD and thank Him because you know by faith that He must have a better purpose for your life? Most of us would say, "How could this happen to me? I've been good, LORD!" Then we would dive into self-pity, proceed to worry our heads off, and have a private nervous breakdown. If we respond to our tests like that, we are acting in the same pattern of unbelief that caused the Israelites to fail to trust God in one trial after another.

But on the other hand, God has provided for us all of these biblical case histories so that we can learn from their mistakes. He has also given us precious promises for all our needs.

PROMISES FOR THE WORRY ADDICT

Listen to some of the specific promises the LORD has given us regarding worry:

Cast all your anxiety on Him because He cares for you. (1 Peter 5:7)

Your responsibility: cast your anxieties upon the LORD. *His promise*: He will carry them for you because He cares for you.

Stop worrying about anything, but in everything, by prayer and petition, with thanksgiving, present your requests to God. And the peace of God, which transcends all understanding, will guard your hearts and your minds in Christ Jesus. (Philippians 4:6–7 HL)

Your responsibility: stop worrying and commit everything to the LORD in prayer with thanksgiving. *His promise*: He will give you His supernatural peace.

And my God will meet all your needs according to His glorious riches in Christ Jesus. (Philippians 4:19)

Your responsibility: trust Him with your needs. *His promise*: He will supply all your needs according to the measure of Christ's wealth.

All these promises are either true or they're not. God cannot lie. He has to keep His promises to us. And the LORD has given us every reason to know that He cares for us and will keep His promises.

When I was a young believer and just learning about trusting God instead of worrying, I suddenly became ill and was hospitalized. I found that I couldn't be released until my entire bill was paid. The bill was several hundred dollars. My total assets were just over seventeen dollars in my bank account. With a big grin on my face, I wrote a check for that entire amount and sent it to my church via a friend. You see, just before this happened, I had learned this promise: **"'Bring the whole tithe into the storehouse, that there may be food in my house. TEST ME IN THIS,' says the LORD Almighty, 'and see if I will not throw open the floodgates of heaven and pour out so much blessing that you will not have room enough for it.'"** (Malachi 3:10)

I wasn't making a deal with the LORD. I simply believed that He would take care of my needs. I had also recently learned: **"Remember this: Whoever sows sparingly will also reap sparingly, and whoever sows generously will also reap generously. Each man should give what he has decided in his heart to give, not reluctantly or under compulsion, for God loves a cheerful [hilarious] giver."** (2 Corinthians 9:6–7)

The answer was almost immediate. A friend from work visited me to say that the boss had discovered I'd been given a raise three months before, but it had not been put into effect because of an accounting office error. He gave me a check for the amount due. It was much more than I needed for the hospital bill!

Just listen to the logical reasons God gives to prove His care for us: **"He who did not spare His own Son, but delivered Him up for us all, how will He not also with Him freely give us ALL THINGS? . . . For if while we were enemies, we were reconciled to God through the death of His Son, MUCH MORE, having been reconciled, we shall be saved [daily] by His life."** (Romans 8:32; 5:10 NASB) God's logic is this: if He loved us enough to give the most for us when we were His enemies, what will He do for us now that we are His children? The answer—*much more!*

THE SIN THE LORD COULD NOT FORGIVE

The LORD overcame and forgave that generation some awful sins. They were guilty of idolatry, adultery, an orgy, rebellion against God's appointed leaders, constant griping, and more. All of these things did not stop God from working with them, nor did they cause Him to revoke His promises. The one sin that the LORD holds up as the cause of their rejection in the Epistle to the Hebrews is their refusing to believe His promises.

It was a truly serious matter when God, using this Exodus generation as a warning to us, said,

Therefore, let us FEAR lest, while a promise remains of entering His rest, any one of you should seem to have come short of it [fail to claim it]. **For indeed we have had good news** [of entering God's rest by faith] **preached to us, just as they also; but the word they heard did not profit them, because it was not united by faith in those who heard. For we who have believed enter [His] rest.** (Hebrews 4:1-3 NASB)

That generation failed to mix God's promises with faith. It's comparable to having a warehouse full of concrete. It is useless for construction until we take it out and mix it with water and gravel. The promises do us no good unless we get them out of the Bible, into our heads, and believe them when the appropriate situation arises in our life.

GRACE UPON GRACE

Meanwhile, back at the Sinai, the LORD once again in pure grace provided for the Israelites in spite of their unbelief. That evening He rained so much quail upon the entire camp that the birds were coming out of their nostrils. The next morning, He rained a perfect food upon the people. When the Israelites came out of their tents, rubbing the sleep from their eyes, they spotted this waferlike food all over the ground and said in Hebrew, *"Manna?"* which means, "What is it?" The LORD displayed His sense of humor when He had them call His food "What is it?" They ate "what is it" for the next forty years.

The patience and grace of our God is so beautifully demonstrated by the way He treated this generation. The Bible says, **"The Israelites ate manna forty years, until they came to** a land that was settled; they ate manna until they reached the border of Canaan." (Exodus 16:35) The LORD continued to provide this heavenly food, even though later they began to grumble about the lack of variety in their diet.

Moses and Aaron did seek to get the Israelites straightened out about who they were really grumbling against: ". . . the LORD has heard your grumbling against HIM. Who are we? You are not grumbling against us, BUT AGAINST THE LORD." (Exodus 16:8 HL) It is imperative to remember that our griping and complaining about life is actually griping against the LORD. And our worrying is in reality saying that the One who died for us doesn't care about us.

NO WATER

After many days, the people came to Rephidim (17:1), which means "refreshments." Once again, the LORD gave them another important opportunity to learn to believe His promises. He intended for this to be an occasion in which their souls would be refreshed through learning a valuable lesson of faith. Had they believed His promises, it would have been just that for them.

We read that they camped there and there was no water. Once more, they refused to mix the promises of God with faith. Instead, they *meribah'd* against Moses. This Hebrew word shows a new dimension of their unbelief. It comes from a root that means "to argue with contempt." They displayed contempt for Moses, and also tested the LORD in an especially presumptuous way by saying, "Is the LORD among us or not?" This was really a stupid question to raise in the light of their situation. It's pretty hard to ignore a constantly present pillar of cloud by day and pillar of fire by night, wouldn't you say?

A SMITTEN ROCK THAT BECAME A SPRING

This time Moses became exasperated with the people. He told the LORD, ". . . a little more and they will stone me."

(Exodus 17:4 NASB) So the LORD gave him some unusual orders. He told Moses to go out in front of them. Moses probably thought, "LORD, are you trying to get me killed? If I go before these irrational people, I'll become a better target for their rocks."

But the LORD showed Moses a rock and said, **"'I will stand there before you by the rock at Horeb. Strike the rock, and water will come out of it for the people to drink.' So Moses did this in the sight of the elders of Israel."** (Exodus 17:6) This is a beautiful type of the LORD Jesus' redemptive work. With the angel of the LORD standing before Moses by the rock, Moses couldn't hit the rock without striking Him first. And remember, the angel of the LORD in the Old Testament was the preincarnate Christ. The Holy Spirit makes this clear when He said through Paul, **". . . for they drank from the spiritual rock that accompanied them, and that rock was CHRIST."** (1 Corinthians 10:4) As soon as Moses struck the rock, water came gushing out. This is a picture of the LORD Jesus Christ being smitten for our sins, so that the Holy Spirit could be poured out upon all of us who believe.

SOME SAD LESSONS

The LORD really gave that generation "the water treatment." First, there was too much water at the Red sea. Second, there was poison water at Marah. Third, there was no water at Rephidim. You would have thought that the Israelites would have finally wised up to these tests and trusted the LORD. But instead, they continued in unbelief. By this time, their repeated refusal to believe the LORD's promises had become a deeply ingrained habit.

They continued the pattern of unbelief even as the LORD gave them many more gracious opportunities to trust Him. They failed all of the tests of faith while at Mount Sinai receiving the Law. They also failed to believe the LORD while en route from Mount Sinai to the border of the promised land. Though they were God's children, their hearts were hardened against walking by faith.

There are so many believers in the Church today who are

not walking by faith and depending upon the Spirit. They are on the way to heaven, but without reward. They are destined to live a defeated, unhappy and unfulfilled life in the wilderness of carnality—unless they begin to believe the promises of God. **So, as the Holy Spirit says: "Today, if you hear His voice,/do not harden your hearts as [they did at the Meribah],/during the time of testing in the desert,/where your fathers tested and tried Me/and for forty years saw what I did."** (Hebrews 3:7–9)

The LORD was seeking to get the Israelites to believe Him in "smaller matters," so they could trust Him in the "giant crisis."

CHAPTER THIRTEEN

Grasshoppers or Giants?

As a man thinks in his heart, so he is.
Proverbs 23:7 HL

It was about fourteen months from the time the Israelites left Egypt until they arrived at the borders of the promised land. The LORD had taken them on a long route in an attempt to train them in combat faith. The extended time also allowed for the giving of the Law, and all the orders of sacrifice and worship.

Now at last they were at the border of the land that had been promised to them by an oath of the LORD. The LORD wanted them to have evidence of the wonders and fruitfulness of the land. So the LORD said to Moses, **"'Send some men to explore the land of Canaan, which I AM GIVING to the Israelites. From each ancestral tribe send one of its leaders.'"** (Numbers 13:1-2)

Moses sent twelve leaders, one from each tribe, into Canaan to do a complete military reconnaissance of the land, and also to report on its general condition. Moses wanted to form a plan of attack from their report so they could go in at once and possess it.

After forty days they returned and brought with them evidence of its prosperity and a report of its fortifications and people. One bunch of grapes they brought back was so large that it took two men to carry it on a pole between them. (Today this is the official emblem of the Israeli Ministry of Tourism!)

THE MAJORITY REPORT, PART 1

The twelve men began to speak in glowing terms about the incredible fertility and richness of the land. It was just as the LORD had described—"it flowed with milk and honey." (Imagine that!)

But in the midst of this good news, ten of the men introduced the first word of unbelief:

BUT the people who live there are powerful, and the cities are fortified and very large. We even saw descendants of Anak [an ancient race of fierce giants] **there. The Amalekites live in the Negev; the Hittites, Jebusites and Amorites live in the hill country; and the Canaanites live near the sea and along the Jordan.** (Numbers 13:28–29)

There they go again! The pattern of unbelief these men cultivated during the deliverance from Egypt and the trip through the desert took over. Their analysis of the situation was totally from the human viewpoint. Their lack of faith immediately infected the rest of the people. The LORD had promised them the land would be beautiful and rich. Since that proved to be true, why couldn't they believe the rest of God's promise in which He committed Himself to give them the land?

THE MINORITY REPORT, PART 1

Two of the twelve men, however, had finally cracked the faith barrier and were living by combat faith. By that kind of faith Caleb and Joshua presented the Divine viewpoint of their scouting mission. I like to call them "the Valiant Two."

Listen carefully to their beautiful statement of the DVP: **"Then Caleb quieted the people before Moses, and said, 'We should by all means go up at once and take possession of it,**

for we are certainly able to conquer them.'" (Numbers 13:30 HL literally, from the Hebrew) Now the Valiant Two saw the same details and obstacles the others did. But they looked at them through God's promise to fight for them and give them the land. They also remembered how the LORD had fought for them against the impossible odds at the Red sea. So in their minds, giants were child's play for the power of God that they had already seen displayed.

THE MAJORITY REPORT, PART 2

But the "Doubting Ten" interrupted Caleb and said,

"We can't attack those people; they are stronger than we are." And they spread among the Israelites a bad report about the land they had explored. They said, "The land we explored devours those living in it. All the people we saw there are of GREAT SIZE. We saw the Nephilim there (the descendants of Anak come from the Nephilim). We seemed like GRASS-HOPPERS IN OUR OWN EYES, and we looked the same to them." (Numbers 13:31–33)

This is probably the most classic statement of the human viewpoint in the entire Bible. With a mental attitude like this, a person is defeated before he starts. If we see ourselves as "grasshoppers," then that is the way we will act. And you can rest assured others will agree with our self-evaluation.

YOU ARE WHAT GOD SAYS YOU ARE!

In any kind of pursuit in life, our mental attitude is an essential key to success. But in combat, whether physical or spiritual, it is a matter of life and death. Our "positive" mental attitude must come from the confidence of knowing that God keeps His promises to those who are *in His will*. God's character is at stake when it comes to keeping His Word—it is simply impossible for God to lie.

139

The Bible teaches us what we are because of our spiritual birth and union with Christ. Most of the Epistles begin by stating what God has made us because of our position *in Christ*. Because of this exalted position, we are declared to be the righteousness of God (2 Corinthians 5:21), justified (Romans 5:1), sanctified and redeemed (1 Corinthians 1:30), freed from all condemnation (Romans 8:1), forgiven of all sin (Colossians 2:13–14), made a totally new creation (2 Corinthians 5:17), given a new self, created in the image of God (Colossians 3:10), given an inheritance that cannot be taken away (1 Peter 1:4), accepted in the Beloved, and so on.

These things are already absolutely true of us because God says they are. However, we don't usually feel like they are true when we first read about them. Sometimes I have thought, "Is God trying to mock me? I don't feel like a new creation in whom old things have passed away and new things have come." But my error was *going by my feelings*. The things God declares to be true of me because of my position in Christ only become true *in my experience* when I count them true by cold-blooded faith.

God says, **"Do not lie to one another since you laid aside the OLD SELF with its evil practices, and have put on the NEW SELF who is being renewed to a true knowledge according to the image of the One who created him."** (Colossians 3:9–10 NASB) We put on the new self by counting true what God says of us, then the Holy Spirit makes it a reality in our lives.

We are also promised victory over the enemy giant within,

> **. . . knowing this, that our old self was crucified with Him, so that our body of sin might be rendered powerless, in order that we should no longer be slaves to the sin nature; for he who has died is freed from the sin nature . . . Even so *consider* yourselves to be dead to the sin nature, but alive to God in Christ Jesus. . . . For the sin nature shall not be master over you, for you are not under law, but under grace.** (Romans 6:6–7, 11, 14 HL)

The Holy Spirit gives us victory over the sin nature as we consider (by faith in what God says) ourselves to be dead to the sin nature's power and alive in Christ's resurrection life in which sin has no authority to rule. What we count as true becomes true. Our mental attitude, which is based on the promises of God's Word, gives the victory. The Christian life is a matter of constantly becoming what *we already are in Christ* through claiming what God says.

What we are in Christ is not a myth, or something we imagine ourselves to be. Be warned that there is a vast difference between the kind of mental attitude produced by the Holy Spirit, and what is being peddled in the Church by some men who have fallen in techniques borrowed from the world. There is a form of positive thinking that works, to a certain degree, by mobilizing the goal orientation of the mind. This technique enables "the flesh to try harder." Such techniques do not depend upon the LORD for their power, but upon human ability. They are, therefore, totally in error and contradictory to the most basic teaching of the Word of God concerning living for God.

THE PLAGUE OF THE HUMAN VIEWPOINT

Let us quickly review how Israel's unbelief developed into a mental attitude of defeat.

When Moses first came with promises and signs from God for Israel and the straw for making bricks was taken away, they said, "'May the LORD look upon you and judge you! You have made us a stench to Pharaoh and his [servants] and have put a sword in their hand to kill us.'" (Exodus 5:21)

When tested at the Red sea, they said to Moses,

> "Was it because there were no graves in Egypt that you brought us to the desert to die? What have you done to us by bringing us out of Egypt? Didn't we say to you in Egypt, "Leave us alone; let us serve the Egyptians"? It would have been better for us to serve the Egyptians than to die in the desert!" (Exodus 14:11–12)

When tested at the bitter waters of Marah: **"So the people grumbled against Moses, saying, 'What are we to drink?'"**

When tested with no food,

The whole community grumbled against Moses and Aaron. The Israelites said to them, "If only we had died by the LORD's hand in Egypt! There we sat around pots of meat and ate all the food we wanted, but you have brought us out into this desert to starve this entire assembly to death." (Exodus 16:2–3)

When tested with no water at Rephidim: "So they quarreled with Moses and said, 'give us water to drink.' . . . Then Moses cried out to the LORD, 'What am I to do with these people? They are almost ready to stone me.'" (Exodus 17:2, 4)

When Moses was on Mount Sinai receiving the Law from God: "When the people saw that Moses was so long in coming down from the mountain, they gathered around Aaron and said, 'Come make us gods who will go before us. As for this fellow Moses who brought us up out of Egypt, we don't know what has happened to him.'" (Exodus 32:1)

After they ate for a while the bread which God sent them daily from heaven,

The rabble with them began to crave other food, and again the Israelites started wailing and said, "If only we had meat to eat! We remember the fish we ate in Egypt AT NO COST—also the cucumbers, melons, leeks, onions and garlic. But now we have lost our appetite; we never see anything but this MANNA!" (Numbers 11:4–6)

SO WHAT'S NEW?

The Israelites' reaction to the "majority report" about the giants and great fortified cities shouldn't be a great surprise at all, should it? Here is how they reacted to their final test of faith:

That night all the people of the community raised their voices and wept aloud. All the Israelites grumbled against Moses and Aaron, and the whole as-

sembly said to them, "If only we had died in Egypt! Or in this desert! Why is the LORD bringing us to this land only to let us fall by the sword? Our wives and our children will be taken as plunder. Wouldn't it be better for us to go back to Egypt?" And they said to each other, "We should choose a leader and go back to Egypt." (Numbers 14:1–4)

Do you see how irrational unbelief can be? Wnen they were at the Red sea they said it would have been better to have remained slaves in Egypt than to die in the desert. Then in the desert they said it would have been better to have died by the LORD's hand in Egypt than to die in the desert. Now at the borders of the promised land they say it would have been better to have died in the desert. These unbelieving rascals didn't want to die anywhere at any time! They just had to find something to gripe about and someone to blame for their lack of faith.

And they finally came out into the open and blamed the whole thing on the LORD, saying that He had brought them to the promised land to kill them by the sword.

THE MINORITY REPORT, PART 2

Even for someone as great as Moses, this kind of unbelief was too much. **"Then Moses and Aaron fell facedown in front of the whole Israelite assembly gathered there."** (Numbers 14:5) This was not unbelief on their part. They were overcome by grief and were interceding for the people so the LORD wouldn't wipe them out.

It took great courage, which only a seasoned combat faith could give, for the "Valiant Two" to stand forth before that panicked mob and challenge their unbelief. If you haven't learned it already, people who are not believing God tend to hate someone who *is* believing Him. An expression of the Divine viewpoint is an automatic reprimand to the one operating in the human viewpoint. This is illustrated all the way through the Bible, but especially right after this minority report.

Listen to this awe inspiring display of combat faith by the Valiant Two:

143

Joshua son of Nun and Caleb son of Jephunneh, who were among those who had explored the land, tore their clothes and said to the entire Israelite assembly, "The land we passed through and explored is exceedingly good. If the LORD is pleased with us, HE WILL LEAD US INTO THAT LAND, a land flowing with milk and honey, and WILL GIVE IT TO US. ONLY DO NOT REBEL AGAINST THE LORD. And do not be afraid of the people of the land, because WE WILL SWALLOW [EAT] THEM UP. Their protection is gone, but THE LORD IS WITH US. Do not be afraid of them." (Numbers 14:6-9)

From us mere humans, there have been only a few statements of the Divine viewpoint as magnificent as this one, such as those made by Moses at the Red sea or David before Goliath. These two men were "flying by instruments." If they had been going by their human senses or emotions, they would have been on their way to points south—fast.

How did this unbelieving group of God's kids receive this demonstration of faith? **"But the whole assembly talked about stoning them."** (Numbers 14:10) If the LORD hadn't intervened, Moses, Aaron, Joshua, and Caleb would have soon been under a pile of rocks. But you know the LORD will *never* let down one of His children who is believing and standing on His promises. Sometimes, it is God's will for a believer to seal his testimony of faith by dying as a martyr. In that case, God gives a special grace of courage and confidence to the one believing Him. But if that time has not come, the child of God is indestructible, no matter what the odds.

ONE MAN AND GOD ARE A MAJORITY!

Probably one of the big reasons I'm still alive, not to mention still in the ministry, is because of an old Jewish prayer warrior named Mae Walker. I'm sure she is with the LORD now. When I was a young believer at Berachah Church in

Houston, she adopted me as her spiritual son. She not only prayed for me without ceasing, but taught me a tremendous amount about the Divine viewpoint of life.

She used to sit me down in front of her wheelchair and look at me with her piercing eyes and say, "Hal, don't you ever be afraid of the crowds. One man and God are a majority!" From her wheelchair, in great pain, she taught me more than anyone else about praising the LORD in all things, and trusting God even while being opposed on every side.

God used her to help me believe Him and to overcome my great fear of speaking before crowds. I had an unnatural timidity and fear of performing in any capacity before people. God once again showed His sense of humor in sending me into some of the toughest witnessing situations imaginable.

It was Mae Walker's training in faith that later enabled me to boldly proclaim the message of Christ to the hostile college audiences of the 1960s and early 1970s. I was terrified just speaking before friendly, sympathetic groups. But the LORD sent me before audiences that were 99 percent hostile and in some cases physically violent.

It was this faith that gave me the boldness to preach to a hostile group of communist students at Simon Frazier University in Canada. The head of the local Communist party at the University was the first one to come forward and accept Christ. He later became the boldest Christian youth leader in the area.

It was this same faith that gave me the courage to take over a Students for a Democratic Society (SDS) meeting at the University of California at Berkeley and challenge the group to the claims of Christ, even though some visiting members of the Popular Front for the Liberation of Palestine threatened to kill me on the spot. This resulted in many young freshmen coming to Christ instead of being hoodwinked by the SDS into Marxism.

The Majority Is Usually Wrong!

In spiritual matters, history shows that the majority has almost always been wrong. So don't follow a teaching simply because those around you are believing it. Check it out with the Word.

In comparison with the three and a half million unbelieving Israelites of the Exodus, good old Moses, Aaron, Caleb, and Joshua plus God were definitely the majority!

UPWARD TO THE PINNACLE OF FAITH

In the midst of the threat to stone him, Moses rose to heights of faith exceeded only by our LORD Jesus Christ. God said of the unbelieving majority,

> **"How long will these people treat Me with contempt? How long will they refuse to believe in Me, IN SPITE OF ALL THE MIRACULOUS SIGNS I HAVE PERFORMED AMONG THEM? I will strike them down with a plague and destroy them, but I will make you into a nation greater and stronger than they."** (Numbers 14:10–11)

Now why do you think the LORD proposed this to Moses? We know the LORD doesn't go back on an unconditional covenant. That would contradict His attribute of *immutablity*. Nor did He need Moses to explain to Him the implications of destroying the nation. That would have contradicted His attribute of *omniscience*. Prophecy would have been completely invalidated because God had promised He would bring the twelve tribes descended from Abraham, Isaac, and Jacob into Canaan. That would have contradicted His attribute of *veracity*. If He had wiped them out, His character would have been compromised. *This God cannot do!* The whole basis of one of the greatest single acts of faith ever attained by a man is Moses' knowledge of and faith in the character of God, and his single-minded concern for God's glory.

This was a great personal test for Moses. First of all, it was a tremendous test of his ego. It could have been a heady wine for him to think about being the founding father of a new nation of God's people. This test demonstrated that Moses was concerned only for God's glory, not his own. This is true humility.

Second, it was a great test of Moses' forgiveness and love. These people had maligned his character in every way. They had filled his life with trials. They had tried to kill him on several occasions. If Moses had been out of fellowship with the LORD, it would have been sweet revenge to see those miserable unbelieving people wiped out.

But instead, Moses flew by instruments right into the heavens of God's eternal glory. There were giants around that day, but they didn't measure up to Moses' big toe.

Moses stood in the breach as a great high priest that day, interceding for God's wayward children. This is a good picture of what our LORD Jesus does for us each day in the presence of the Father (1 John 2:1-2). He is our "defense attorney," who has already paid the full penalty for every charge that can be brought against us. Because of this, the Scripture tells us our defense attorney will never lose a case for anyone who believes in Him: **"Hence, also, He is able to save forever those who draw near to God through Him, since He always lives to make intercession for them."** (Hebrews 7:25 NASB)

Read carefully what Moses prayed:

Moses said to the LORD, "Then the Egyptians will hear about it! . . . They have already heard that You, O LORD, are with these people and that You, O LORD, have been seen face to face, that Your cloud stays over them, and that You go before them in a pillar of cloud by day and a pillar of fire by night. If You put these people to death all at one time, the nations who have heard this report about You will say, 'The LORD was not able to bring these people into the land He promised them on oath; so He slaughtered them in the desert.'

"Now may the LORD's strength be displayed, just as YOU have declared: 'The LORD is slow to anger, abounding in LOVE and FORGIVING sin and rebellion. . . .' In accordance with YOUR GREAT

LOVE, forgive the sin of these people, just as You have pardoned them from the time they left Egypt until now." (Numbers 14:13-19)

TRUE INTERCESSORY PRAYER

Moses demonstrated the principles of real intercessory prayer. First, he appealed on the basis of all the things the LORD had done on behalf of the Israelites that linked His name to theirs. These mighty deeds had already been reported among the nations. God's reputation was at stake.

Second, he reminded the LORD that He had promised these people on oath to give them the land of Canaan. The nations were also aware of this promise. They could say that if the LORD was that committed to these people, He must be too weak to fulfill His promise to them.

Third, Moses appealed to the LORD on the basis of the direct personal revelation He gave to him concerning His character. At Mount Sinai, Moses had asked to see God's glory. The LORD told Moses that He would pass before him, but cover him in the cleft of a rock until He had passed by, so he could see only His back. For, God said, no one could see His face and live. Then the LORD proclaimed His name to Moses:

And He passed in front of Moses, proclaiming, "I AM WHO I AM (Jehovah, Jehovah), the COMPASSIONATE and GRACIOUS God, SLOW TO ANGER, ABOUNDING IN LOVE and FAITHFULNESS, MAINTAINING LOVE to thousands, and FORGIVING wickedness, rebellion and sin." (Exodus 34:5-6 HL)

This is the revelation of the attributes of God's character on which Moses stood by faith in his prayer. In essence, Moses told God, "LORD, You *cannot* wipe out these Israelites. This would be in contradiction to all of Your attributes, which You revealed to me." How about that? Do you know something? God just loves to test us and have us tell Him, on the basis of a mature knowledge of His revealed character, "LORD, You cannot do this, because it would contradict who *You are*." That is real combat faith in intercession.

FORGIVEN BUT DISQUALIFIED

The LORD replied to Moses' prayer,

"I have forgiven them, as you asked. Nevertheless, as surely as I live and as surely as the glory of the LORD fills the whole earth, not one of the men who saw My glory and the miraculous signs I performed in Egypt and in the desert but who disobeyed Me and TESTED ME TEN TIMES—not one of them will ever see the land I promised on oath to their forefathers. No one who has treated Me with contempt will ever see it." (Numbers 14:20–23)

These people absolutely and categorically refused to learn how to believe the LORD's promises. Ten times they specifically tested the LORD with their unbelief. As a believer, it is possible to harden your heart against trusting the LORD in daily living. This is what the writer to the Hebrews was warning about when he said,

Who were they who heard and rebelled? Were they not all those Moses led out of Egypt? And with whom was He angry for forty years? Was it not with those who sinned, whose bodies fell in the desert? And to whom did God swear that they would never enter HIS REST if not to those who disobeyed? So we see that they were not able to enter, because of THEIR UNBELIEF. . . . See to it, brothers, that none of you has a sinful, unbelieving heart that turns away from the living God. But encourage one another daily, as long as it is called Today, so that none of you may be hardened by sin's deceitfulness. (Hebrews 3:16–19, 12–13)

If we fail to learn how to believe God's promises from the trials He allows into our lives, we disqualify ourselves from serving Him. God will overcome every sin in our life except one—*unbelief*. For without faith it is impossible to live for God, because unbelief short-circuits the Holy Spirit's power through us. In the light of this, we should never take trials lightly, or fail to see their significance. Instead, we should see them as opportunities to learn how to believe. Then we can even **"rejoice in our sufferings, because we know that suffering produces perseverance; perseverance, character; and character, hope. And hope does not disappoint us, because God has poured out His love into our hearts by the Holy Spirit, whom He has given us."** (Romans 5:3–5)

THE REWARD OF FAITH

Whereas all of the people who refused to believe God's promises lived short unfulfilled lives of anxiety and drudgery, the LORD said to the faithful few, **"'But because My servant Caleb has a different spirit and follows Me wholeheartedly, I will bring him into the land he went to, and his descendants will inherit it.'"** (Numbers 14:24)

Forty-five years later, after Caleb had fought for five years to liberate land for the other tribes, he finally came to the Judean land of the giants and said to Joshua

> **"You know what the LORD said to Moses the man of God at Kadesh Barnea about you and me. I was forty years old when Moses the servant of the LORD sent me from Kadesh Barnea to explore the land. And I brought him back a report according to my convictions, but my brothers who went up with me made the hearts of the people melt with fear. I, however, followed the LORD my God wholeheartedly. So on that day Moses swore to me, 'The land on which your feet have walked will be your inheritance and that of your children forever, because you have followed the LORD my God wholeheartedly.'**
>
> **"Now then, just as the LORD promised, He has**

kept me alive for forty-five years since the time He said this to Moses, while Israel moved about in the desert. So here I am today, eighty-five years old! I am still as strong today as the day Moses sent me out; [I'm just as vigorous to go out to battle now as I was then]. Now give me this hill country that the LORD promised me that day. You yourself heard then that the Anakites were there and their cities were large and fortified, but, the LORD helping me, I will drive them out just as He said." [The Divine viewpoint just gets stronger in those who develop a pattern of believing God's promises.]

Then Joshua blessed Caleb son of Jephunneh and gave him Hebron as his inheritance. So Hebron has belonged to Caleb son of Jephunneh the Keniz-zite ever since, because he followed the LORD, the God of Israel, wholeheartedly. (Hebron used to be called Kiriath Arba after Arba, who was the greatest man among the Anakites.) Then the land had rest from war. (Joshua 14:6–15)

Caleb believed "the bigger they are, the harder they fall" when the LORD is with you. He defeated the giants in short order. By faith, Caleb, at eighty-five, defeated Arba, the chief and mightiest warrior of the Anakim, in personal combat. (This is how David a few centuries later got the idea that God was in the giant-killing business. He read about how his great-great-great-great-uncle Caleb defeated the giants of the area where he was born. David, as a little shepherd boy, believed God's Word literally. So God made him Israel's greatest king and warrior, and the sweet psalmist of Israel.)

The True Fountain of Youth

Caleb also found the coveted fountain of youth—it's called "resting in the LORD." While the unbelieving wasted away and died in that terrible Sinai desert with worry and anxiety, Caleb stayed young and grew stronger by focusing his faith toward the promised land and resting in the LORD. In our modern fast-paced society that is filled with anxieties, everyone tries to cling to their youth as long as possible. Millions of dollars are spent annually on cosmetics, special spas, health food, fitness programs, and so on so people can hold on to a youthful appearance. But the most destructive factor that causes rapid aging and loss of health is the worry and anxiety caused by our generally godless and materialistic society. These have been traced out as the major causes of many severe illnesses. So learning to "crack the faith barrier" and to live by faith actually helps keep one young and healthy. Caleb certainly demonstrated that for all of us to follow.

THE REAL TRAGEDY OF IT ALL

The real tragedy of the rejected generation came into clear focus when the new generation forty years later approached the land and sent two spies into Jericho. When they talked to a hooker named Rahab, she said,

> **"I know that the LORD has given this land to you and that A GREAT FEAR OF YOU has fallen on us, so that all who live in this country are melting in fear because of you. We have heard how the LORD dried up the water of the Red sea for you when you came out of Egypt . . . When we heard of it** [forty years earlier], **our hearts melted and everyone's courage failed because of you, for the LORD your God is God in heaven above and on the earth below."** (Joshua 2:9–11)

One of the reasons the LORD took His time bringing His people to the borders of Canaan was to let the news of the Red sea reach the Canaanites so that they would be terrified and demoralized. That information reached the people of Canaan within at most two months. If that first generation had simply marched in by faith and said, "Boo," the giants would have fled in terror. God had already prepared the way for victory. But that generation operated "by sight and not by faith."

CHAPTER FOURTEEN

The Real War

For our struggle is not against flesh and blood, but against the demon rulers, against the demon authorities, against the powers behind this dark world system and against the spiritual forces of evil who even operate in the heavenly realm.

Ephesians 6:12 HL

In our study of how God trained the Israelites during the Exodus, one thing comes through loud and clear: He often deliberately led them into humanly impossible situations to teach them how to believe His promises so that they would grow to maturity. As we have seen, this is one of the major reasons God allows trials in our life. As soon as we believe the LORD's promises, we are sustained in the midst of these trials and they are removed when the lesson of faith is learned.

However, there are some other significant reasons why we may experience trials and suffering. We are caught in the middle of an ancient conflict between the LORD and His archenemy, the Devil. We are involved in a real and active war in this life that is fought on three fronts. We face the very real enemies of Satan, the world system, which is controlled by Satan, and the flesh or sin nature. To win against these formidable enemies requires personal combat training. Each one of these enemies is superior to all our human resources. We can

153

only win the battle by using the strength, weapons, and motivation provided by God. We can only be protected and survive by putting on the armor provided by God.

THE ANCIENT CONFLICT

Down through the ages, man has pondered the question of why there is suffering, especially when it falls upon people who seem to be moral and good. The problems of sicknesses, crippling diseases, injuries, birth defects, and calamities (both natural and man-made) have troubled mankind and defied human attempts to explain them.

The Bible has always had the only true and helpful explanation of these issues, although man has rarely taken it to heart.

THE BEGINNING OF SORROWS

All suffering directly or indirectly comes as an inevitable consequence of man's original rejection of God and the loss of relationship with Him. Mankind was originally created perfect and was placed in a paradise where his every conceivable need was provided. He had a relationship with God and was designed to find fulfillment and function properly, only through fellowship with Him.

For this reason, Man was created in the image of God. He had will, intellect, emotion, moral reason, and everlasting existence. All of these attributes have to do with his immaterial being, which is called the soul.

Man was given will or volition so that he could choose to love God and have fellowship with Him. He was given intellect so that he could understand God's revelation to Him. He was given emotion so that he could respond to God's love. Apart from these factors, especially freedom of choice, true love and fellowship are impossible, so God took a calculated risk and created them in man. Without freedom of choice, man would have been no more than a robot.

But the risk was that man could reject his relationship

with God and go his own way into destruction. The very attributes that give man the capacity for relationship and fellowship with God also give him the *capacity for great evil*. To illustrate, a beautifully designed jet aircraft is a dangerous machine if it loses its communication and navigational instruments in heavy-overcast weather. The plane will still fly perfectly, but it will surely crash.

In a much more critical way, man was created to function properly only in a relationship with God. The spiritual nature originally created in man was the communication and guidance system that made him able to have an intimate relationship with God. But if man chose to reject God by disobeying Him, the spiritual nature would immediately die, making a relationship with God impossible.

Man was given only one test of his relationship with God: **"'You are free to eat from any tree in the garden; but you must not eat from the tree of** [which gives] **the knowledge of good and evil, for in the day you eat of it you will surely die.'"** (Genesis 2:16–17 NASB)

The Hebrew term for **knowledge** used here means an "experiential knowledge." Adam had a theoretical knowledge of good and evil. But he actually had to sin in order to **experience** the knowledge of good and evil.

There were many factors involved in this test. First, there was trust. It was not explained to Adam why the test was given. He was simply told the consequences of the choice: instant death and an experiential knowledge of good and evil. This required him to trust that God would not lie to him, and that He was not withholding anything from him that was in his best interest.

Second was the factor of man's relationship with God. Death meant separation from God. The Hebrew literally says, "dying you shall surely die." The original act of sin actually brought about two deaths. When Adam chose to eat of the tree that gave the knowledge of good and evil, he died instantly in his spirit, and as a direct consequence, his physical process of death began.

LIKE BEGETS LIKE

Spiritual death and its consequences were inevitably passed on to all the descendants of Adam and Eve. Like can only produce like. Our first parents' sin caused the whole human race after them to be born spiritually dead and separated from God. In this condition, cut off from the only One who could guide and empower him to live correctly, man plunged out of control into sin, and its inevitable consequence—suffering and death.

Each descendant of Adam and Eve is born with a fallen nature, which gives him a great and fearful inclination toward cruelty, evil, and inhumanity. Of the first two children born to Adam and Eve, one, motivated by jealousy, murdered the other in a cool, calculated way. This revealed the inherited effects of the fall to be immediate and terrible.

The history of man ever since then has been a continuous horror story of murder, war, the conquest of the weak by the strong. War is the chief legacy of human history. Its bloody trail is woven through the fabric of virtually every generation, proving that mankind has a mega-malfunction in his nature.

This is not to say that there aren't some noble and merciful characteristics in fallen man. But given the right circumstances, the old sin nature will take over the best of mankind. If you don't believe this, just remember that Hitler's Germany was made up of some of the most educated and cultured people of this "enlightened" century.

Just think for a moment what would happen in New York, Chicago, Los Angeles, or any large city, if the police force were disbanded.

As the Oxford University professor and philosopher C. S. Lewis once observed, "Education and culture has only tended to make man a more clever and sophisticated devil." When the restraints of civilization and law enforcement break down, man turns to the law of the jungle.

About one hundred years ago science boasted that it would solve all of man's problems and bring in a millennium of world peace and prosperity. But instead, it has mainly brought man more efficient weapons of destruction. With the existing number of thermonuclear-tipped ballistic missiles and weapons of chemical warfare, science has made it possible for people bent upon conquest (and every generation has had its ample quota of these) to wage a war that would virtually annihilate all life on planet earth. If some do survive, they will surely envy the dead. Jesus the Messiah predicted this very condition would develop just before His return: **"'For then there will be great distress, unequaled from the beginning of the world until now—and never to be equaled again. If those days had not been cut short, no one would survive, but for the sake of the elect those days will be shortened.'"** (Matthew 24:21-22) This is the first time in history that mankind possesses the weapons needed to fulfill this prophecy.

The record of history proves that the most dangerous being on planet earth is man. Man himself, separated from God, has been the cause of the death and suffering of more fellow human beings than all other sources combined.

THE GREAT CAUSE OF HUMAN SUFFERING

How did man become what he is? The four consequences of the fall of man—spiritual death, separation from God, the inherited evil nature, and Satan's authority over mankind and planet earth—combine to make the greatest sources of human suffering.

Wars, murders, selfishness, robbery, human-inflicted injuries, and so on, are all directly caused by the inherited sin nature. The Bible speaks extensively about this condition:

What causes fights and quarrels among you? Don't they come from your desires that battle within you? You want something but don't get it. You kill and covet, but you cannot have what you want. . . . (James 4:1-2)

Jesus called the crowd to Him and said, "Listen to Me, everyone, and understand this. Nothing outside a man can make him 'unclean' by going into him. Rather, it is what comes out of a man that makes him

157

'unclean.' . . . For from within, out of men's hearts, come evil thoughts, sexual immorality, theft, murder, adultery, greed, malice, deceit, lewdness, envy, slander, arrogance and folly. All these evils come from inside and make a man 'unclean.'" (Mark 7:14–15, 21–23)

The heart is more deceitful than all else and is desperately sick; Who can understand it? (Jeremiah 17:9 NASB)

> There is not a righteous man on earth
> who [always] does what is right and
> never sins. (Ecclesiastes 7:20)

This condition is totally unreformable by human means. Religion can never change the sin nature, or "flesh," as it is sometimes called in the New Testament. Religion works to modify behavior from the outside. Thinking it will modify the sin nature is like expecting a just washed pig never to return to the mud. Scrubbing the pig's exterior may give you a clean pig for a while, but it will never change its basic nature. God doesn't attempt to change man from the outside, or even to reform the old sin nature on the inside.

The LORD Jesus proclaimed the only cure for this condition. Jesus Christ said to a very devout, sincere religious man,

Unless a man is born from above, he cannot perceive the kingdom of God. . . . That which is born of the flesh is physical, but that which is born of the Spirit is spiritual. Stop marveling that I said, "You all [referring to all the religious leaders of Israel] must be born from above." (John 3:3, 6–7 HL)

Without this spiritual birth, fellowship with God is impossible. But we cannot be reborn spiritually until the debt of sin, which caused the death of our human spirit, is paid. And just as a choice to reject fellowship with God was made, so a choice must be made to re-establish fellowship. Jesus taught this as He described how to be born again: "'For God so loved the world that He gave [to die for our sins] His one and only Son, [in order] that whoever believes in Him shall not perish but have eternal life.'" (John 3:16)

Eternal life is the same kind of spiritual life that God has. The spirit that died in the fall is recreated in us by the Holy Spirit at the moment of saving faith. This enables the believer to perceive and know God so that fellowship is once again restored. For God is spirit and we must have the same kind of life to have a relationship with Him.

WHY MAN WAS CREATED

The greater question underlying the issue of why there is evil and suffering comes into focus when we examine how man originally fell into sin. Eve was tempted directly and Adam indirectly by a super being known as Satan and the Devil.

This angelic being is described as having been the most beautiful, intelligent, and powerful being God ever created. He was also the most honored of all creatures.

He was the guardian of the holiness of God's throne and thus in the closest and most intimate relationship with the Tri-une God (Ezekiel 28:11–15).

He was known as Lucifer ("The Shining One") until he sought to take over God's throne and become like God himself (Isaiah 14:12–14). This is when sin first entered the universe. Lucifer became known as Satan and led a third of the angelic creation into his rebellion against God.

Apparently, God gave Satan and his angels time to repent, but they did not do it. So God pronounced upon them the judgment of eternal separation from His presence. When God pronounced this sentence, Satan apparently accused Him of being unjust and unloving. Though God was under no moral necessity to do so, He elected to demonstrate to both the angels that remained faithful and the fallen angels (now also known as demons) the perfection of His justice and the enormity of His love.

Thus began "operation planet earth." God created a creature called man who was vastly inferior to angels in power, mobility, and intelligence. But man had one thing in common with the angels—the image of God in his immaterial being. It was in this common area of free choice, intelligence, emotion, and moral reason that God set up a test to demonstrate fully His attributes of justice and love.

SATAN WON THE FIRST BATTLE

Satan and his angels have been given, as it were, a suspended sentence until operation planet earth is concluded. In this state of temporary freedom, Satan and his demons are doing everything possible to thwart God's purpose with man in a kind of perverted hope that they can win a reprieve from God's judgment.[1] The very fact that Satan and his fallen angels are involved in an all-out assault against us should make us welcome God's combat training.

ROUND ONE

Satan won the first round by taking over a serpent (which was the most intelligent and beautiful of all animals before the fall) and through it persuaded Eve and Adam to believe a lie about God's character. He then appealed to their pride by promising that the knowledge of good and evil would make them like God. As a result, Eve, and then Adam, rejected God's Word, disobeyed God's one command, and plunged headlong into sin, separation, and death.

When this occurred, Adam, who had been entrusted with the title deed to the earth, automatically gave Satan legal ownership and authority over the earth and mankind. This is why the LORD Jesus called Satan **"the ruler of this world."** (John 12:31 NASB) It is also why Satan made this insolent boast: **"The Devil led [Jesus] up to a high place and showed Him in an instant all the kingdoms of the world. And he said to Him, 'I will give you all their authority and splendor, for it has been given to me, and I can give it to anyone I want to.'"** (Luke 4:5–6) Jesus did not challenge Satan's boast, because

God must be just, and honor even the Devil's legal rights.

The frightful truth is this: **"We know that we are children of God, and that the whole world is under the control of the evil one."** (1 John 5:19) In other words, when we become children of God, we become aliens in enemy territory.

The LORD Jesus not only purchased our redemption at the cross, but also legally won back the title deed to the earth. Yet He will not exercise His right of ownership until the Second Coming, when He will bind Satan for a thousand years and set up God's kingdom on earth over which He will personally rule as Israel's Messiah. Until then, we live in a Satan-controlled world and we are subject to attacks from him and his demon army. Satan is a determined and powerful enemy who is totally dedicated to our defeat and destruction.

SATAN'S STRATEGY

His first objective is to keep as many as possible from being saved. God says, **"And even if our gospel is veiled, it is veiled to those who are perishing. The GOD OF THIS AGE has blinded the minds of unbelievers, so that they cannot see the light of the gospel of the glory of Christ, who is the image of God."** (2 Corinthians 4:3–4) As discussed at length in my book *Satan Is Alive and Well on Planet Earth*,[2] I believe Satan is convinced that he can win an acquittal from judgment by causing so many humans to be lost that God would bend His justice and not judge them. In Satan's reasoning, once a precedent is set with mankind, God would have to do the same for him and his demons.

His second objective is to neutralize, and if possible destroy, a believer. Once we are lost to Satan's kingdom, he focuses his attack on preventing us from walking by faith, since it is the most essential key for living and serving God effectively. In connection with this, Satan especially seeks to keep us from learning and believing God's Word. This is why we *must* get a combat knowledge of God's word. The LORD says that He gave gifted teachers and pastors,

> **. . . so that the body of Christ may be built up until we all reach unity in the faith and in the knowledge**

of the Son of God and become mature, attaining to the whole measure of the fullness of Christ. Then we will no longer be infants, tossed back and forth by the waves, and blown here and there by every wind of teaching and by the cunning and craftiness of men in their deceitful scheming. (Ephesians 4:12–14)

These two objectives of Satan are the source of a great deal of man's sufferings and trials. Jesus warned that we would suffer trials inspired by Satan:

If the world hates you, keep in mind that it hated Me first. If you belonged to the world, it would love you as its own. As it is, you do not belong to the world, but I have chosen you out of the world. That is why the world hates you. Remember the words I spoke to you: "No servant is greater than his master." If they persecuted Me, they will persecute you also. . . . All this I have told you so that you will not go astray. (John 15:18–20, 16:1)

Our LORD never promised freedom from persecution, but rather offers inner joy, peace, and excitement even in the midst of it.

GOD HAS WON THE GREAT BATTLE

When Satan led man into rejecting his relationship with God, it appeared that he had not just won a battle, but the whole war. However, this tragedy became the opportunity for the greatest display of God's justice and love.

God fully vindicated His justice by not compromising it even to save man. Instead, God upheld both His infinite righteousness and justice when He Himself became a man and bore the penalty of His own law, which had been violated by man.

God also demonstrated His infinite love in this same act

by dying for the very creatures who had rejected Him and had become His enemies.

Every time a man believes in Messiah Jesus as Savior, or a Christian under trial believes God's promises, the angels of God rejoice.

Why do they rejoice? Why do angels intently watch how man responds to God with his volition? The LORD Jesus said,

"I tell you that in the same way there [is] more rejoicing in heaven over one sinner who repents than over ninety-nine righteous persons who do not need to repent. . . . In the same way, I tell you, there is rejoicing in the presence of the ANGELS of God over one sinner who repents." (Luke 15:7, 10)

Peter spoke of the angels' constant observation of how God deals with man:

It was revealed to them [the prophets] that they were not serving themselves but you, when they spoke of the things that have now been told you by those who have preached the gospel to you by the Holy Spirit sent from heaven—things into which the ANGELS continually look intently. (1 Peter 1:12 HL)

Daniel the prophet also spoke of a special order of angels: **"'I was looking in the visions in my mind as I lay on my bed, and behold, an ANGELIC WATCHER, a holy one, descended from heaven.'"** (Daniel 4:13 NASB) This order of angels apparently does nothing but observe all human beings continuously. This is why some of the decisions made and acts of faith done by a person when there are no other human witnesses are the most important to God. As I once heard a minister say, "A secret sin on earth is an open scandal in heaven." And also, "A secret act of faith on earth is an open celebration in heaven."

The angels of God rejoice whenever man trusts the LORD because it vindicates God's justice in condemning Satan and his angels. Every time man, who is vastly inferior in attributes and knowledge of God to the angels, chooses for God, it proves that God was just in that condemnation.

The principle of faithfulness in secret is beautifully illustrated in the case of David. It was his faithfulness in little things, where only God saw him, that prepared him to conquer Goliath.

As the LORD Jesus said, **"He who is faithful in a very little thing will be faithful also in much; and he who is unrighteous in a very little thing will be unrighteous also in much."** (Luke 16:10 NASB) This is why He also said, **"Many who are first** [in the eyes of man] **will be last; and the last first."** (Matthew 19:30 NASB)

IS GOD UNFAIR?

Both the angels of God and the demons are learning about the infinite perfections of God's character through His dealings with mankind. Some might say that God is unfair to involve us in His ancient conflict with the fallen angels. But people who are tempted to think this way do not take into account the indescribable glory and eternal rewards God has waiting for those who by faith endure trials and remain faithful. And the LORD God promises, **"No temptation has seized you except what is common to man. And God is faithful; He will not let you be tempted beyond what you can bear. But when you are tempted, He will also provide a way out so that you can stand up under it."** (1 Corinthians 10:13)

Not many believers are called upon to endure direct satanic attack in the way that Job was. Only those who are specially prepared and called are thrust into that conflict. But rest assured that these battle-tested warriors will be given special eternal rewards.

CHAPTER FIFTEEN

The Weapons of Our Warfare

For the weapons of our warfare are not of the flesh, but divinely powerful for the destruction of fortresses. We are destroying speculations and every lofty thing raised up against the knowledge of God.
2 Corinthians 10:3–4 NASB

Since we are aliens at war in enemy territory from the moment we are born into God's eternal family, we must consider God's provisions for fighting and winning that war. Faith is the only acceptable means we have for appropriating our strength, weapons, and armor for the battle in which we have been placed.

THREE-DIMENSIONAL WARFARE

Our warfare is being fought on three fronts: the flesh or sin nature, the Devil, and the world system which he controls. God has given us special equipment and means for fighting in each of these areas, and awesome strength to empower us for the battle.

Some may say, "I don't want to be in this battle." But you

only have two choices. Either you will count for God and receive eternal rewards, or you will be sidetracked, neutralized, and made miserable through little-understood enemies. Whether we like it or not, we are all in the war. One of the biggest problems we face today is that some believers don't even want to know who their enemies are. Many would rather not talk about Satan, feeling that if they do, this will somehow bring him glory. Others are so frightened of him they argue that if you ignore him, he will go away. Still others don't want to admit his existence and possible threat to the believer.

THE FILLING OF THE SPIRIT, OUR SOURCE OF POWER

The enemies we face are so powerful that only God the Holy Spirit can enable us to overcome them. The Apostle Paul spoke of the Holy Spirit when he revealed the source of power behind his incredible ministry: **"And for this purpose also I labor, striving according to His power, which MIGHTILY WORKS WITHIN ME."** (Colossians 1:29 NASB)

JESUS CHRIST IS OUR MODEL

Even the LORD Jesus depended upon the Holy Spirit to empower and to work through His human nature while He voluntarily lived on earth under the limitations of being a true man. He kept saying in various ways throughout the Gospel of John, **"I can do nothing of Myself."** (See John 5:19, 30; 8:28; 12:49; 14:10) When Jesus began His messianic ministry, the source of His power was clearly stated: **"And Jesus, FULL OF THE HOLY SPIRIT, returned from the Jordan."** (Luke 4:1 NASB) **"And Jesus returned to Galilee IN THE POWER OF THE SPIRIT."** (Luke 4:14 NASB) The LORD Jesus also applied a prophecy concerning the Holy Spirit to Himself: **"THE SPIRIT OF THE LORD IS UPON ME, because He anointed Me to preach the gospel to the poor."** (Luke 4:18 NASB)

The wonderful mystery of the person of the LORD Jesus while He was upon earth is that even though He had the power in His Divine nature to perform any of His miracles, he voluntarily laid aside the use of His power to depend upon the Holy Spirit, who dwelt within His humanity. This He did in order to qualify as a true human being, because only a true man could die for the sins of other men.

We must understand this truth to comprehend the greatest promise that Jesus made to us: **"Truly, truly, I say to you, he who believes** [keeps on believing] **in Me, the works that I do shall he do also; and greater works than these shall he do; because I go to the Father** [to send back the Holy Spirit to dwell in us]." (John 14:12 NASB) Jesus made this promise because He was about to send upon those who believe in Him the same Holy Spirit who empowered His human nature to live for God. The *greater* works refer to greater quantity, not quality. While Jesus was upon the earth, the Holy Spirit only filled His human nature. After He successfully atoned for our sins and ascended to the Father, He sent the Holy Spirit back to take up permanent residence in every believer, so that the Holy Spirit can now produce the same kind of works in much greater numbers.

As we keep on depending upon Christ, the Holy Spirit sustains, guides, and empowers us to live as He lived. He produces the life of Christ *in* us. Now we can perform the same kind of mighty works that He did, *if* we are filled with the Spirit.

THE WAR AGAINST THE FLESH, AND THE FILLING OF THE SPIRIT

The filling of the Spirit only becomes possible after we make a once-and-for-all decision to give the title deed of our life to Christ. This is a prerequisite to receiving His filling and empowering ministry.

The Indwelling of the Spirit

We must realize that every believer today is *indwelt by the Holy Spirit* from the moment of salvation. After a short transition period of the initial giving of the Holy Spirit that was recorded in the book of Acts, the norm became this: **"However, you are not in the flesh but in the Spirit, if indeed the Spirit of God dwells in you. But if anyone does not have the Spirit of Christ, he does not belong to Him."** (Romans 8:9 NASB) This shows that it is impossible to be a Christian today and not be indwelt by the Holy Spirit. He takes up permanent residence in each believer.

There are two important truths to draw from this. First, since the Holy Spirit now lives in every believer, it is possible for us to live a supernatural life for God that was not available to the Old Testament saints.

Second, even though the Holy Spirit does dwell in every Christian, we are not filled with the Holy Spirit until we learn and believe the instructions and promises of the Word of God concerning this indispensable ministry.

The Filling of the Spirit and Spiritual Gifts

It is also important to distinguish between the Spirit's ministry of filling and the gifts of the Spirit. The *filling* is the Spirit's ministry by which He gives us victory over the sin nature and its temptations, teaches us, guides us, and empowers us for service. It is appropriated by faith on a moment-by-moment basis. An act of known disobedience to God's will causes us to lose the filling until we repent, confess the sin, and believe God again.

On the other hand, a spiritual gift is a God-given ability to serve in a specific area in accordance with God's plan for your life. The Holy Spirit sovereignly distributes the gifts (1 Corinthians 12:11). Every believer receives at least one spiritual gift (1 Peter 4:10). Gifts are given for life. Even carnality doesn't cause us to lose them (Romans 11:29). Most important, according to 1 Corinthians 13:1–8, it is possible to exercise our spiritual gifts without manifesting the most important fruit and evidence of being filled with the Spirit, which is *love*.

The gifts of the Spirit do not give us victory over the flesh, only the filling ministry does. This is clearly evidenced by the fact that it is possible to **"speak with the tongues of men and**

even angels, and not have love." (1 Corinthians 13:1) No spiritual gift gives us the filling of the Spirit, it must be appropriated moment by moment by faith.

The Filling of the Spirit and Maturity

We are either filled with the Spirit at any given moment, or we are not. However, maturity is a process that occurs over a period of time. There is no such thing as "instant maturity." As we have seen, God uses trials as a part of our maturing training program.

Maturity has to do with our *knowledge* of God's Word, our *wisdom* in applying what we know to our experience, our level of *faith* or ability to believe God, our consistency in *obeying* God, our development of *proven character*, and our *production* level in the will of God.

The filling of the Spirit takes us at whatever level of maturity we are and empowers us to serve effectively and live for God. The more mature we are, the more the Holy Spirit has to work with, and the more His fruits of love, joy, peace, patience, kindness, goodness, faithfulness, gentleness, and self-control are manifest in us (Galatians 5:22–23 NASB).

The Filling of the Spirit Is Not a Mutual Assistance Program

One of the greatest hindrances to being filled with the Spirit is the natural inclination of the flesh to try and help God live the Christian life. God does not "help those who help themselves!" This is such a subtle trap that the LORD has provided a special kind of training to teach us how to depend only upon the Spirit, and not our human abilities. Remember how Moses had to be broken of self-confidence and taught God-confidence! God doesn't do away with our human talents and abilities, He simply takes them over in the yielded believer and makes them effective through the Holy Spirit's control.

God led the Apostle Paul to share his personal experience of how he learned to depend upon the Holy Spirit and not himself. He shows that the law was given as God's instrument to teach us how to be filled with the Spirit. The following is an analysis of this experience. I call it *God's law school*.

First, *the law was given to teach us what sin is*. As Paul said, **"I would not have come to know sin except through the Law; for I would not have known about coveting [lusting] if the Law had not said, 'You shall not covet.'"** (Romans 7:7 NASB) Paul learned about the most subtle form of sin from the law after being born again and indwelt by the Holy Spirit. The tenth commandment is the only one that doesn't deal with outward behavior, but rather deals with the *inner thoughts and motivations*. All Paul's life before he was born spiritually, he sought to order his *outward behavior* by the law. Paul gave this testimony concerning his religious life prior to meeting Christ:

> **If anyone else thinks he has reasons to put confidence in the flesh** [human ability], **I have more: . . . [I was] a Hebrew of Hebrews; in regard to the law, a Pharisee; as for zeal, persecuting the church; as for legalistic righteousness, FAULTLESS. But whatever was to my profit I now consider loss for the sake of Christ. . . . that I may gain Christ and be found in Him, not having a righteousness of my own that comes from the law, but that which is through faith in Christ—the righteousness that comes from God and is by faith.** (Philippians 3:4b–9)

But after Paul's conversion, his new spiritual nature, illumined by the indwelling Holy Spirit, became sensitive to the sinfulness of his thoughts and motives, not just his outward conformity to the man-made traditions added to the law by a false form of Judaism.

This was the whole point of the Sermon on the Mount. Jesus was seeking to convince those smug and self-satisfied religious leaders that their lawkeeping was only dealing with the outer behavior, not the motives of the heart. This was the reason behind Jesus saying to them later,

> **"Woe to you, teachers of the law and Pharisees, you hypocrites! [For] you are like whitewashed tombs,**

which look beautiful on the outside but on the inside are full of dead men's bones and everything unclean. In the same way, on the outside you appear to people as righteous but on the inside you are full of hypocrisy and wickedness." (Matthew 23:27–28)

This is the essence of all "religion." It cleans up the outside, but it cannot clean up the inside. Christianity is not a religion, but a personal relationship and communion of life with God based upon the perfect atoning work of Christ and the indwelling Holy Spirit. True Christianity cleans up the inside. Only the Holy Spirit can clean up our hearts and empower us to live the kind of life God can approve.

Second, *the law was given to stir up our sin natures and make us sin more* (Romans 7:8–14).

Most Christians balk at this point, even though it is clearly taught in the Bible. Paul said, **"I was once alive apart from the Law, but when the commandment came, sin** [the sin nature] **became alive, and I died."** (Romans 7:9 NASB) Here Paul speaks of being alive in Christ and rejoicing in his new life until he started to try and keep the law. Then the trouble really started. The law actually provoked his old sin nature, with which we are all born, into action. The new nature, with its supersensitive conscience, began to condemn the bad thoughts and desires, which had formerly been rationalized away by his religious traditions. The very law that Paul had once thought was the source of life he now found to be a source of death. There are six different kinds of death spoken of in the Bible. Here it is used to mean losing the communion and intimacy of his moment-by-moment fellowship with God. Paul teaches in his Epistles, particularly in Romans 7 and 8, that being out of fellowship with God is a kind of temporary death.

This experience with the law made Paul aware of a condition to which all men are congenitally blind:

So then, the Law is holy and the commandment is holy, righteous and good. Did that which is good,

171

then become death to me? By no means! But in order that sin might be RECOGNIZED as a sin nature, it produced death in me through what was good, so that through the commandment the sin nature might become utterly sinful. We know that the Law is spiritual; but I am unspiritual, sold as a slave to the sin nature. (Romans 7:12-14 HL)

Paul reveals here that there's nothing wrong with the law, but on the contrary, the law forced him to recognize the utter sinfulness of a sin nature within him through stirring it into uncontrollable action.

Let me illustrate this principle. Let's say that you have two neighbors living at opposite ends of your block, each with large glass greenhouses in their front yards. The neighbor on the east corner puts up a large sign which reads, "Do not throw rocks at greenhouse." The neighbor on the west corner doesn't put up a sign. Now which greenhouse do you think will get stoned first? I can just imagine a few teenagers walking along the street with no thought in the world of stoning anything. Then one of them catches sight of the large sign. Silence . . . One teenager looks at the other, and a little smile comes over his face. A strange nature within begins to rise to the challenge. An exciting strategy of attack is planned and later executed. I don't know about you, but this was common in my neighborhood, when I was a boy. The very neighbor who was perpetually shouting prohibitions and accusations at us was the one whose house always got special attention on Halloween.

This is one of the main reasons why God gave the law. He had to show us how hopeless it is to seek to gain God's acceptance through our human efforts. The Scripture says about this dilemma: **"The law was added so that the trespass [transgression] might INCREASE. But where sin increased, grace increased all the more,"** and, **"The sting of death is sin, and the POWER of sin [the sin nature] is the LAW."** (Romans 5:20 and 1 Corinthians 15:56)

As incredible as it sounds, the law was given to man to make him *sin more*. This was done to make mankind see how hopeless it is to try and earn God's forgiveness and acceptance through human efforts and merit. The sin nature actually gets its power over us through the principle of law, which places us under a merit system that depends upon human ability. The moment we place ourselves under the principle of law, the situation becomes hopeless, because our sin nature cannot be controlled by any form of human ability, no matter how sincerely we try.

This is the very essence of biblical Christianity—the fact that in and of ourselves we can do nothing to help save ourselves or to live the Christian life. If man could have done these things, then Christ died in vain. Either salvation depends upon the LORD, or upon man. The Bible clearly teaches that God does not offer a mutual assistance program for salvation or living the Christian life.

Third, *the law was given to drive us to despair of self effort* (Romans 7:15-24).

We are so blind to our complete inability to live for God that He has to send us through "law school" to break us of the tenacious notion that somehow we can keep the law. We deceive ourselves into thinking that the key to victory is to be more sincere, to be more dedicated, to try harder in the flesh through various self-improvement tricks. But such gimmicks as classes on "positive self-motivation," "positive thinking," "positive self-image," "positive imagery," and "positive confession," if not carefully taught in the light of Scripture, can become substitutes for being filled with the Spirit.

There is a very dangerous form of teaching contained in most of these seminars that has its origin in the New Age Movement. New Age thinking is based on the eastern religious concept of Divine being within everyone, and says we have all that is necessary to live successful "spiritual lives" *within ourselves*. This is the key to discerning the truth from error. Instead of looking *without* to Jesus and inviting Him into our hearts, this counterfeit teaching, which has been cleverly clothed in Christian terminology, instructs us to look *within ourselves* for the power, motivation, and understanding we need to live. This New Age error is subtly being slipped into the Church in the guise of many of the "self-improvement, self-motivation and success-motivation" seminars.

173

The fatal flaw in this doctrine is its teaching that the self has all the powers necessary to be successful in the spiritual realm as well as the secular. It draws upon the teaching of both modern psychology and eastern religion, which allege that there are vast and mysterious untapped powers in the "unused 90 percent of our subconscious minds." The way this is being taught, in most cases, proves to be simply anti-biblical philosophy that strengthens human pride and encourages the self to try harder.

The New Age teaching that says we are all gods has been subtly redefined in "Christian" terms by some in the Church. This teaching reasons that since we were all reborn into God's image, we are therefore little gods capable of "speaking our wills into existence." The obvious error here is that we are declared to be "children of God," never "gods" except in one passage—John 10:34—in which Jesus was subtly bringing a scathing condemnation upon the Jews for not understanding their own Scriptures concerning the Messiah. This teaching makes our wills more important than God's will, and leads to very serious heresy.[1]

There is a proper Scriptural sense in which we are to have a positive mental attitude and a correct self-image: We must saturate our minds with the truth of what *God* says we are *in Christ*, not with various positive confessions that are out of line with His Word. If we keep feeding self with ego-boosting positive affirmations, we are working diametrically against what God has taught in His Word.

The inevitable result of all self-effort to live for God is always this:

For that which I am doing, I do not understand; for I am not practicing what I would like to do, but I am doing the very thing I hate. . . . For the good that I wish, I do not do; but I practice the very evil that I do not wish. . . . I find then the principle that evil is present in me, the one who wishes to do good. For I joyfully concur with the law of God in the inner man, but I see a different law in the members of my body, waging war against the law of my mind, and

making me a prisoner of the law of sin which is in my members. (Romans 7:15, 19, 21–23 NASB)

Have you ever found that the harder you tried to live by the law principle the more miserably you failed? I call this experience "Christian schizophrenia," because the two natures within us (the sin nature and the new spiritual nature) are clearly in opposition to each other. All true born-again believers will experience this struggle between their two antithetical natures.

In these verses, the great Apostle Paul describes his own miserable failure and clearly brings out the basic problem. The principle of law depends upon human ability. The reason we fail to keep the law principle is because it cannot give us the power to do so. It can only demand that we obey. Far from helping us, it only causes our sin natures to rebel. Because of our new spiritual natures, we delight in the righteousness contained in the law, but even our new natures do not have the power in and of themselves to keep God's law.

Paul discovered several very important things in this phase of his "law school" training.

He learned that the *source* of sin was not in his new self, which was created by the new birth, but in his sin nature, which was still present and unreformed within him. He said,

I know that nothing good lives in me, that is, in my sinful nature. For what I do is not the good I want to do; no, the evil I do not want to do—this I keep on doing. Now if I do what I do not want to do, IT IS NO LONGER I WHO DO IT, but it is the sin nature living in me that does it. (Romans 7:18–20 HL)

This taught Paul that human resources could never conquer the sin nature. Even God didn't try to reform it. Instead, He put a new nature within us that is created in His image and constantly desires to follow Him.

Out of this Paul also learned that *he could accept the new self that God had created in Him*. He didn't have to hate his "real self" when he sinned, because it was not the source of the sin.

The Bible tells us that this new spiritual nature never sins: **"No one who is born of God practices sin, because His seed abides in him; and he** [referring to God's seed which is the new nature created within us] **cannot sin, because He is born of God."** (1 John 3:9 NASB) John previously said in the same Epistle, **"If we say that we have no sin, we are deceiving ourselves and the truth is not in us."** (1 John 1:8 NASB) The only conclusion we can draw is that though the Christian still sins, the source is not the new nature, which cannot sin, but the flesh or sin nature still dwelling in him. The new spiritual nature, which is God's seed implanted in our new self, always desires to follow God. In fact, this is the reason a true believer cannot habitually live in sin, because his new nature always wants to follow God who created it in His image. This nature makes a backslidden Christian very unhappy and makes him want to return to fellowship with his Heavenly Father. This is also the source of the conflict described in Romans 7.

Knowing and applying these truths will give you a healthy self-image and true self-worth. You *can* accept the new self, which God created, and reject the old self because it is no longer "the true you." God healed horribly damaged souls through these truths centuries before modern psychology came on the scene. The Bible says, **"If any man is in Christ, he is a new creature; the old things passed away; behold, new things have come."** (2 Corinthians 5:17 NASB) We begin to have mental health when we count these divinely declared facts as true. The most true thing about us is what God says is true about us. This is different from the counterfeit philosophy of the New Agers that have been slipped into the Church. We are to allow our minds to be transformed with what God declares us to be in the Scriptures, not with vain human imaginings designed to prop up the old self and bolster human ego.

God has His own positive mental attitude program. He commands us to count as true that which He declares in His Word is already true of us because of our mystical union of life with Christ. Because we are "in Christ," the Bible says this about us: we have been justified from sin's claims against us and have been raised into a new life over which the sin nature has no authority; we are clothed with God's own righteousness; we are accepted in the beloved; we are seated with Christ on His throne and can by faith exercise His authority; we are co-heirs with Christ; we are holy and without blame. God wants our minds to be programmed with these truths. When we count these facts true, His Spirit makes them a reality in our experience. The Christian life is a matter of becoming by faith what you already are **in Christ**. The LORD does not want us to program our minds with mere human imaginings. His Spirit transforms us into the image of His Son with ever increasing glory as we look into the mirror of His Word and count what it says of us true. (See 2 Corinthians 3:1–18)

After Paul sought with all his human resources to live for God under the law, he was finally plunged into such despair that he said he wanted to die: **"Wretched man that I am! Who will set me free from the body of this death?"** (Romans 7:24 NASB) This was the cry of a desperate man. But from God's perspective, he was finally a candidate for a miracle. His self-confidence was finally broken. Law school had done its work of driving him to despair of human efforts to live for God. That brings us to the ultimate purpose of the law for Christians.

Fourth, *the law was given to drive us to total dependence upon the indwelling Holy Spirit.* (Romans 7:25–8:4)

Paul joyfully proclaims the wonderful liberating answer he found to his desperate question: **"Thanks be to God through Jesus Christ our LORD! . . . There is therefore now no condemnation for those who are in Christ Jesus."** (Romans 7:25a, 8:1 NASB) Victory over the sin nature and the hopeless struggle against it begins with understanding and believing in the perfect completed atoning work of the LORD Jesus. The moment that we received Him and His pardon by faith we were all baptized by the Holy Spirit into a mystical, physical, eternal union with Him (1 Corinthians 12:12–14). From that time onward, we are declared to be **in Christ**. This simple little prepositional phrase, which appears in various forms about 160 times in the New Testament Epistles, declares the most fantastic reality in the universe as far as the believer is concerned. This describes a union that makes us a member of Christ's body, flesh, and bone (See Ephesians 5:30 KJV).

Why the Believer Can Never Be Condemned

Since Christians have been joined into an actual union with Christ, all that is true of Him has become true of us. Jesus Christ has already been condemned for all of our sins, so since we are **in Christ,** we cannot be recondemned for the sins for which He has already fully paid. God wants us to know that the law of double jeopardy applies here—no one can be tried twice for the same crime. When we really understand this truth, we should shout it from the rooftops: **"There is therefore now no condemnation for those who are IN CHRIST JESUS."**

The significance of all this as far as achieving victory over the flesh is concerned is that it gives us the right *motivation* for living for Christ. We don't have to walk in fear of being condemned and disowned for our sins. Satan just loves to get the Christian focused inward upon his sins and failures. A good old guilt trip will paralyze the most sincere and ardent Christian. The only proper motivation for living the Christian life must be to serve the LORD out of a loving and grateful heart for all He has already given. Our motivation must not be duty, obligation, or fear of rejection.

Two Principles of Life Contrasted

Paul reveals the new principle of life which gives us victory:

For the law of the Spirit of [who gives] life in Christ Jesus has set you free from the law of [that produces] sin and death. For what the Law could not do, weak as it was through the flesh, GOD DID: sending His own Son in the likeness of sinful flesh and as an offering for sin, He condemned sin in the flesh, in order that the righteousness required by the Law might be produced IN us, who do not walk according to the flesh [with all its weaknesses], **but accord-**

ing to [the infinite power of] **the Spirit.** (Romans 8:2–4 NASB and HL)

We have been set free from the principle of law as a way of life because obedience to it depended upon our human abilities; it could only produce sin and death.

The principle we are now under works on the basis of a finished atonement that freed the Holy Spirit to permanently dwell in us and produce life and righteousness. He is now free to live permanently in our mortal bodies even though the sin nature, with all its godless lusts, is still present in us. How this was made possible is a very deep truth of the Word of God that is hard to grasp, but God considers it very important for us to understand. You see, the LORD Jesus not only had to die for our acts of sin, but more importantly, He had to die under the judgment due our sin natures. This was even more important because the sin nature is the source of our sinful actions. As long as we are in these unresurrected bodies, the sin nature remains alive. It cannot be destroyed until we either receive a resurrected body, or we are transformed into an immortal body through the rapture.

Therefore God had to provide a just ground upon which His Spirit could come into our bodies and deal with our sin natures on a moment-by-moment basis. This is what is meant by the verse, **"God sent His own Son in the likeness of sinful flesh and as an offering for sin [the sin nature]."** It was by this great atoning act on the cross that "He **condemned sin** [the sin nature] **in the flesh,"** that is, He so judged the existence of our sin nature that it is no longer a barrier to His righteous character. The sin nature has now been judged and paid for so completely that God is now free to dwell in our sinful flesh and deal directly with our sinful natures. Furthermore, the power of the sin nature over us, which was total before, is now broken. We no longer *have* to sin. We can now say *no* to its temptations and the Holy Spirit makes it stick.

Paul says that all of this was done **"in order that the requirement of the Law might be fulfilled in us . . . who walk . . . according to the Spirit."** (Romans 8:4 NASB) This is so exciting. The Holy Spirit is in us for the purpose of conquering our old sin nature with all its lusts and habits. All we have to do is to by faith keep depending upon the Holy Spirit and not our own human strength to deal with the lusts and temptations that come from our sin nature. As we choose moment by moment to depend upon the Holy Spirit, He produces a righteous life in us that is above the law's standard.

This what God meant when He said, **"But the fruit of the Spirit is LOVE, joy, peace, patience, kindness, goodness, faithfulness, gentleness, self-control; against such things THERE IS NO LAW."** (Galatians 5:22–23 NASB) There is no law against these nine fruits that are produced in the Spirit-filled believer because they represent the character of Christ.

The most important fruit produced by the filling of the Spirit is *love*. This is God's kind of love and cannot be produced by human effort. First Corinthians 13 describes this Holy Spirit–produced love in detail; this chapter is a portrait of what a Spirit-filled Christian's life should be.

God's kind of love also causes us to live a life that is above the law's demands:

Owe nothing to anyone except to love one another; for he who loves his neighbor HAS FULFILLED THE LAW. For this, "You shall not commit adultery, you shall not murder, you shall not steal, you shall not covet," and if there is any other commandment, it is summed up in this saying, "You shall LOVE your neighbor as yourself." LOVE does no wrong to a neighbor; LOVE therefore is the fulfillment of the law. (Romans 13:8–10 NASB)

How to Be Filled with the Spirit

Once we understand these principles, being filled with the Spirit is very simple. It is as simple as believing and claiming God's promises about what He will do in us through the Holy Spirit. To be filled with the Spirit means to be controlled, guided, and empowered by the Holy Spirit by our deliberate choice to yield Him our wills and depend upon Him.

Just remember some of these fantastic promises of what

the Holy Spirit will do in the one who is filled with Him by faith:

"I can do all things through Christ Who keeps on strengthening me." (Philippians 4:13 HL) Christ pours His mighty strength into us as we depend upon Him and not ourselves. Remember, the Scripture never suggests, "I can do all things by my own strength through thinking positively and mobilizing the latent, hidden powers of my mind." The Bible teaches **Christ**–confidence, not self-confidence. I can be confident because I know that Christ works through me by the Holy Spirit when I trust Him.

> **But I say, keep walking by the Spirit, and you will not carry out the desire of the sin nature. For the sin nature sets its desire against the Spirit, and the Spirit against the sin nature; for these are in opposition to one another, so that you may not do the things that you please. But if you are being led by the Spirit you are not under the Law.** (Galatians 5:16–18 HL)

We are promised victory over the desires and lusts that come into our minds from the sin nature. It *does not* say that we will not have lusts, but it does promise that we will not fulfill them and sin. Our part is to say *no* to the desires, and then, by faith, to depend upon the Holy Spirit to suppress and put them away.

We are also promised that the Holy Spirit will teach us God's word:

> **"But when He, the Spirit of truth, comes, He will guide you into all the truth; for He will not speak on His own initiative, but whatever He hears, He will speak; and He will disclose to you what is to come"** (John 16:13 NASB)

> **And as for you, the anointing which you received from Him abides in you, and you have no need for anyone to teach you; but as His anointing teaches you about all things, and is true and is not a lie, and**

just as it [He] has taught you, you abide in Him.
(1 John 2:27 NASB)

These promises assure us that when we are Spirit filled, the Holy Spirit will teach us and guide us into its application in our life.

One of the Holy Spirit's main missions is to glorify the LORD Jesus, the Messiah in us. Jesus promised: **"'He shall glorify Me; for He shall take of Mine and disclose it to you. All things that the Father has are Mine; therefore I said, that He takes of Mine, and will disclose it to you.'"** (John 16:14–15 NASB) As the Holy Spirit consistently fills us, He forms Christ in us. He then glorifies the LORD Jesus by manifesting His life through us. Incidentally, this verse also reveals the LORD Jesus' claim of absolute deity. Only one who is God Himself can have all things in common with God!

These are some of the more important promises for us to claim and thus be filled with the Spirit. But now we must go on to one of the other important missions of the Holy Spirit in the Spirit-filled believer. The Holy Spirit gives us the power and wisdom to deal with our arch adversary, the Devil.

THE WAR AGAINST THE DEVIL

The Scriptures reveal that the Devil wages a vicious and relentless war against the Christians. Note this warning: **"Be self-controlled and alert. Your enemy the devil prowls around like a roaring lion looking for someone to devour."** (1 Peter 5:8)

Satan uses a variety of attacks against us. The Devil has carefully planned *schemes* or *strategies* for our destruction (Ephesians 6:11). He *blinds* the minds of the unbeliever (2 Corinthians 4:4). He is a master *deceiver* and *perverter* of God's Word (2 Corinthians 11:3, Luke 4:10–12). He masquerades as an *angel of light*, and has a dedicated corps of ministers whom he energizes to masquerade as *ministers of righteousness* within the Church (2 Corinthians 11:13–14). He is the *father of lies*, and can put lies into a carnal Christian's heart (John 8:44,

Acts 5:3). He *accuses* believers before the throne of God (Revelations 12:10). By God's permission, Satan can torment, severely injure, strike with sickness, and kill believers (Job 1 and 2, Luke 22:31–32, 2 Corinthians 12:7–10, and 1 Corinthians 5:1–5).

In the light of these sobering revelations, we need to know how to appropriate our strength and protection, and how to use our armor. The LORD gives us specific instructions about our strength and armor in Ephesians 6:10–18.

Our Strength

"Finally, be strong in the LORD, and in the strength of HIS might." (Ephesians 6:10 NASB) The command to *be strong* is in the present tense, the passive voice, and the imperative mood in the original Greek. Don't freak out, each of these factors has great significance. First, the present tense means to be *continually* strong. The passive voice means that you, the *subject*, receives the action. The imperative mood means that it is a *command*. Put it altogether and it means, **"Allow yourself to be continually made strong by the LORD in the strength of His might."** We have just studied how this is done through the filling of the Holy Spirit. He strengthens us with the power of *the LORD's might*, which is unlimited. So we don't need to fear Satan when we are filled with the Spirit.

Intelligence Report on Our Enemy

"For our struggle is not against flesh and blood, but against the rulers, against the authorities, against the powers behind this dark world-system and against the spiritual forces of evil in the heavenly realms." (Ephesians 6:12 HL) God reveals that Satan has a highly organized army of fallen angels who have different ranks, assignments, and functions. They are deployed so that they secretly control the world-system and its rulers. These evil spirit beings are even in the heavenly realm where God dwells (See Job 1–2).

Checking Out Our Armor

With such a lethal and organized army against us, God commands us to: **". . . put on the full armor of God, so that when the day of evil comes, you may be able to stand your ground, and after you have done everything, TO STAND."** (Ephesians 6:13)

The Belt of Truth

When the Apostle Paul wrote this Epistle, he was chained day and night to one of Caesar's elite household guards. He used the Roman soldier's armor and weapons to illustrate ours. He led most of these soldiers to Christ, as revealed in Philippians 4:21–22.

". . . buckle the belt of TRUTH around your waist." (Ephesians 6:14a HL) The most important part of the Roman soldier's armor was the belt. It was six to eight inches wide, and he attached his body armor and weapons to it. If his belt slipped in battle, he would become vulnerable.

Our belt is the truth of God's Word. All our combat equipment stands or falls with it. The truth refers specifically to our knowledge and understanding of the Bible. A soldier could not wait until he was already in a battle to put on his belt. Neither can we wait to learn a combat knowledge of the Scripture.

The Breastplate

". . . with the breastplate of RIGHTEOUSNESS in place." (Ephesians 6:14b) The breastplate was made of bronze backed with tough pieces of leather. This protected the soldiers' most vital organs. If a blow got through in this area, it was fatal.

Our most vital spiritual areas are guarded by the certainty of the righteousness of God that was given us on the basis of faith alone. **"He made Him [Christ] who knew no sin to be sin on our behalf, that we might become the righteousness of**

God IN HIM." (2 Corinthians 5:21 NASB) We stand against the accusations of Satan in God's righteousness, not our own. This keeps the Devil from dealing us a mortal blow with guilt and doubt.

The Shoes

". . . and having shod your feet with the preparation of the gospel of peace." (Ephesians 6:15 NASB)

Anyone who has fought in any form of hand-to-hand combat knows the importance of having a shoe that gives sure footing. I was once floored in a boxing match because my foot slipped while I was throwing a punch. The other fighter instantly connected with a stunning blow because I was off balance and couldn't dodge it.

The Roman soldier was issued hobnail sandals so that he could keep a sure footing. When you're fighting with swords, your first slip is usually your last.

In our battle with the Devil, sure footing is even more important. He knows how to take advantage of any slip that throws us off balance. Our footing is secured by the previous preparation of the good news concerning peace. This is what we've been studying in this book—how to have inner peace in the midst of trial through God's rest. We prepare for this by memorizing and learning to believe God's promises.

The Shield

"In addition to all this, take up the shield of faith, with which you can extinguish all the flaming arrows of the evil one." (Ephesians 6:16)

The shield, about two feet wide by four feet long, was used by soldiers to ward off thrusts of the enemy's sword as well as volleys of arrows. It was the maneuverable part of the armor that covered wherever it was needed.

The maneuverable part of our armor is faith. Faith stands in the gap wherever defense is needed against the wiles of Satan. Faith defends us against his attacks of temptation, guilt, false doctrine, doubt, misunderstanding, and so on. Our faith in God's character and His word is more than enough to protect us against the evil one's flaming arrows.

The Helmet

"Take the helmet of salvation . . ." (Ephesians 6:17a)

The helmet protected the head. Our spiritual helmet must protect our minds from the lethal blows of Satan's vicious attacks against our salvation. One of the most important aspects of our defense is our firm faith in eternal security.

We need to know from God's word that our salvation doesn't depend upon our performance. It depends upon the finished work of Christ, who purchased forgiveness for our sins past, present, and future. God offers no salvation that is not eternal; for salvation does not depend on man either before or afterward. **"For it is by grace you have been saved, through faith—and this [is] not from yourselves, it is the gift of God— not by works, so that no one can boast."** (2:8–9)

The continuance of our salvation depends upon the high priestly ministry of Christ. About this God swears, **"Therefore He is able to save forever those who come to God through Him, because He always lives to intercede for them."** (Hebrews 7:25) According to this verse, the only way a believer could be lost is for the risen Christ to die!

Satan loves to take obscure verses and passages out of context, and hurl them at the believers. He also uses some ministers to promote the perpetual insecurity of God's children. I have met too many Christians who are on the edge of nervous breakdowns because they are terrified that they have committed some unpardonable sin.

Many others are neutralized because they're laboring to serve God with the wrong motive of trying to keep themselves saved. Satan dances for joy at this kind of confusion caused by twisted Scripture. He always tries to knock off our helmets of security in our salvation. Keep yours on firmly.

Our Sword

". . . and [take] the sword of the Spirit, which is the word of God." (Ephesians 6:17b)

The sword is an offensive weapon. The Roman sword was called a *machaira* and it had a revolutionary design. Its blade was only twenty-four inches long. It was sharpened on both sides and sharply pointed on the end. This design was extremely effective because of the careful and extensive training the Roman legionnaire was given in its use. He could thrust and cut with his sword from any position so that he was never off balance or out of position.

Opposing soldiers of that day all had large swords that were usually sharp on one side. The soldier had to cock his arm and swing at the opponent in a chopping motion. The Roman soldier would duck, catch his enemy off balance and finish him before he could cock his arm for another swing.

Our sword, in the hands of a properly trained believer, never leaves us off balance or out of position. The sword of the Spirit is the word of God that has been learned in a combat knowledge. I mean by this that we must learn Scripture doctrinally to be able to use it effectively when under attack. A doctrine is simply all the Bible says on a given subject, organized in a logical manner so that it can be remembered and used when needed. I used to memorize the main passages on a given doctrine and write a summary next to it. Then I would letter in all the parallel passages. This was one of the most important disciplines the LORD ever gave me. It has saved me in many battles.

Jesus used the sword of the Spirit in this sense when He was tempted by the Devil in Luke 4:1–13. He quoted verses to Satan that exactly countered the temptations he hurled at Him.

Sharpen your sword and practice using it!

Prayer, Our Heavy Artillery

"And pray in the Spirit on all occasions with all kinds of prayers and requests. With this in mind, be alert and always keep on praying for all the saints." (Ephesians 6:18)

In modern warfare, the enemy can be kept at bay and routed by bombardment with heavy artillery. We can do the same with our prayer life. We are to pray, filled with the Spirit, so that He can guide us in God's will and cause our prayers to be on target. We can also protect our flanks by praying for our fellow believers.

Having Prepared, Be Ready To Fight!

". . . and after you have done everything, . . . STAND!" (Ephesians 6:13b)

The Scriptures speak of the evil days, and of specific days when evil comes into our lives (Ephesians 5:15–18, 6:13). This refers to times of personal attack by the Devil. We must not give him a ground of authority in our lives by shrinking back in doubt, fear, and unbelief. And above all, we must not be walking in the flesh. We must face Satan filled with the Spirit and with our armor on.

We are to stand in the courage of faith and the confidence of our position in Christ when attacked by Satan. **"Resist him [Satan], standing firm in the faith . . ."** (1 Peter 5:9) **"Submit yourselves . . . to God. Resist the devil, and he will flee from you."** (James 4:7)

COMBATING THE WORLD-SYSTEM

The last dimension in which we fight is the world-system. The Greek word, *kosmos*, which is translated as "world" in the New Testament, conveys three ideas in its verb form: to put things in order, to systematize, and to adorn or decorate. The noun *kosmos* is carefully defined in the New Testament to describe a world-system, beautifully organized and arranged to function without God, opposed to all that is true in Jesus Christ.

The world-system is presented as adorned with the beautiful concepts of culture, music, art, philosophy, knowledge, social concerns, programs of welfare, science, politics, religion, and pleasure. It embraces all these things in an orderly system. These are not necessarily evil in themselves, but Satan weaves them into a world order so that he can take man's heart away from a true relationship with God and center him on those things that are both temporal and material.

The Battle for Our Affections

Behind all that is tangible in the world-system there is the intangible genius of Satan, the master deceiver. Behind the things of this world is the mastermind who uses them to shift our focus from devotion to Christ to devotion to things. Once this is done, the inevitable ever-increasing force of greed sets in automatically. Because things can never take the place of fellowship with God, we are never satisfied. The more we get, the more we want. James warns of this terrible progression of lust for things:

> **What causes fights and quarrels among you? Don't they come from your desires that battle within you? You want something but don't get it. You kill and covet, but you cannot have what you want. You quarrel and fight. You do not have, because you do not ask God. When you ask, you do not receive, because you ask with wrong motives, that you may spend what you get on your pleasures.**
> **You adulterous people, don't you know that friendship with the world [system] is hatred toward God? Anyone who chooses to be a friend of the world [system] becomes an enemy of God. (James 4:1-4)**

Worldliness Defined

John warns us of the dangers of "worldliness":

> **Do not love the world [system] or anything in the world [system]. If anyone loves the world [system], the love of the Father is not in him. For everything in**

the world [system]—the cravings of sinful man, the lust of his eyes and the boasting of what he has and does—comes not from the Father but from the world [system]. (1 John 2:15–16)

Satan goes all out to alienate our affections from our heavenly Father. Worldliness is putting anything before Christ. It is to become more attached to things than to Him. This is why we must guard our hearts by being filled with the Spirit and being occupied in our hearts with the LORD Jesus. We must meditate upon Him in the Scriptures to keep our affections burning. The main defense against the lure and pull of the world-system is a fervent love for Christ.

The Delicate Line

There is a very delicate line between having the things of this world and the things having you. It is not wrong to have things and wealth. Some of God's greatest servants were wealthy. Wealth only becomes wrong when it is made the chief object of our affections and a primary goal of our life. The Scripture says,

People who WANT to get rich fall into temptation and a trap and into many foolish and harmful desires that plunge men into ruin and destruction. For the LOVE of money is a root of all kinds of evil. Some people, EAGER FOR MONEY, have wandered from the faith and pierced themselves with many griefs. (1 Timothy 6:9–10)

As these verses make clear, it is the motive that makes money and riches wrong. It is the *desire* to get rich, the *love* of money and *being eager* for money that is the source of the problem.

There are two errors to avoid here. One is to teach that it's wrong to have any money or possessions. The other is to teach that we are somehow not believing God if we are not wealthy. The latter is the message of the new "Health and Wealth Gospel." I have been greatly grieved to see some brothers' ministries neutralized by the pursuit of wealth. Once again, it's a fine line we have to walk between having wealth, and wealth having us.

The LORD tells us what our attitude should be: **"But godliness with contentment is great gain. For we brought nothing into the world, and we can take nothing out of it. But if we have food and clothing, we will be content with that."** (1 Timothy 6:6–8)

If the LORD chooses to bless us with wealth, then we should gratefully receive it, and remember that "a man can receive nothing unless it is given him from above." We should use it liberally to help those who are in need. We should also be constantly aware that if we cross that fine line and begin to be attached to riches and things, they will pull our hearts away from devotion to the LORD.

FINAL BRIEFING

These are the enemies and the weapons we have to combat them. May the LORD fill you with His strength, teach you His Word, and protect you with single minded devotion to Him.

CHAPTER SIXTEEN

Why Do Christians Have Trials?

Consider it pure joy, my brothers, whenever you face trials of many kinds, because you know that the testing of your faith develops perseverance.

James 1:2–3

There are two extremes to avoid when approaching the subject of trials. The first is to think that God in His desire to see us grow will constantly bombard us with all kinds of trials. The other is to think that there will be no trials in the life of someone who really has faith and walks with God.

NEED WE FEAR TRIALS?

In answer to the first extreme, the LORD never puts us through more than we can bear. Nor does He give us more testing than is necessary to train our faith for our particular calling. *Only those who are greatly used are greatly tested.* And in those cases, the LORD gives such grace that they are filled with rejoicing in the midst of their trials.

Just look at Paul and Silas's experience at Philippi (see

Acts 16:11–40). They were totally committed to their mission of founding churches. They were walking by faith and were in this city in response to a direct vision from the LORD Jesus Himself. They were courageously witnessing in the face of dangerous opposition.

After much sacrificial labor, they had only two converts— a traveling saleswoman and a formerly demon-possessed fortune-telling slave girl. As a result of delivering the slave girl from her demon of fortune telling, her master had them brutally beaten with the Roman cat-o'-nine-tails and thrown into the lower dungeon of the jail. The lower dungeons were usually filthy, wet, and filled with large rats.

How would you have responded to this situation? Most of us would have sunk into a massive depression and self-pity. We would probably have said, "LORD, I don't deserve this. There I was, boldly witnessing for You. I barely had enough to eat. I was walking with all my heart in obedience to Your Word. And to top it all off, I came here because You appeared to me in a vision and told me to come. And after all this sacrifice, You let me get my back beaten to shreds and my body put into chains in this lousy dungeon where I can't even run from the rats. What kind of a God are you, anyway?"

But what did Paul and Silas do? With their backs raw and bleeding, their muscles aching from their being chained in an uncomfortable position in a damp dungeon, *they sang praises to the LORD at the top of their voices*! And the LORD answered this incredible display of combat faith with an earthquake that shook the whole region, shattered their chains, and flung open the prison doors. Praise Jesus, one way or another He will always respond to His children who praise Him in the midst of unexplainable trials.

As a result, the head jailer, all his family, and most of the prisoners came to know the LORD Jesus as their Savior. These became the charter members of the Philippian Church, which became characterized by rejoicing in the midst of trials. It was all made possible because Paul and Silas walked by faith and not by sight.

This incident illustrates how those who are tested for the ministry's sake are given special grace, if they trust the LORD.

They are not miserable and frightened, but excited and filled with inner joy, sensing the LORD's personal presence and knowing that their life is counting for eternity.

DO COMMITTED AND SPIRITUAL PEOPLE HAVE TRIALS?

It may sound strange to even raise such a question, but this brings us to the second extreme that must be avoided. No one particularly likes trials, and certainly no one should seek them. But as we have examined many biblical case histories, we have seen that those who are truly serving the LORD will experience some tests and trials.

Some ministers with great followings teach that if you are truly walking by faith and making a "positive confession of faith," you are rejecting trials and suffering, you will not experience them. This teaching attributes all or most of the trials, sufferings, sicknesses, and in some cases even poverty to a lack of faith, to "a negative confession," or to unconfessed sin. While it is true that in some cases these conditions can bring about trials, it is certainly not true in every case. These teachers, perhaps unwittingly, have neglected to consider an enormous part of the Scripture in order to establish their doctrine. It is difficult to combat these teachings because they mix some truth with a lot of error. We never want to discount what is true, but we must be discerning and balanced. We must always filter a teaching through the grid of *all* of God's Word. In this chapter I will seek to present a balanced view on the subject, using the *whole* counsel of God, not just selected-proof texts.

GOD'S LOVE FOR EACH BELIEVER

We must always remember that overriding every circumstance that touches our lives is God's deep love and compassion for each one of us. Remember how much grace and love the LORD demonstrated toward the Israelites of the Exodus even though they continued to disbelieve His promises. In reality, they always believed the worst about God's character. In spite of this, God kept delivering them and providing for their every need.

Listen to how the Psalmist perceived the enormity of God's love for the Exodus generation,

> **For they did not believe in God**
> **or trust in His deliverance.**
> **Yet He gave a command to the skies above**
> **and opened the doors of the heavens;**
> **He rained down manna for the people to eat,**
> **he gave them the grain of heaven. . . .**
>
> **In spite of all this, they kept on sinning;**
> **in spite of His wonders, they did not**
> **believe. . . .**
> **Yet He was merciful;**
> **He [atoned for] their iniquities and did not**
> **destroy them.**
> **Time after time He restrained His anger**
> **and did not stir up His full wrath.**
> **He remembered that they were but flesh . . .**
> (Psalms 78:22–24, 32, 38 39)

THE ETERNAL PERSPECTIVE

The Father always views our lives from the perspective of eternity. Our perspective of life is usually most concerned with immediate circumstances.

Christianity has been heavily criticized in recent times for promising "pie in the sky by-and-by." Karl Marx emphasized this kind of reasoning when he called religion "the opiate of the people." He looked on Christians with contempt because they by faith endured sufferings and didn't just live for the material world. He felt that the Christian faith contributed to their passive acceptance of oppression by "the rich capitalists." The record of history, however, shows that men committed to Christian ethics and morality brought about some of the greatest reforms for the poor of the industrial age.

Still Christianity, without apology, does primarily base its hope on eternity. God said through the Apostle Paul, **"If only for this life we have hope in Christ, we are to be pitied more than all men."** (1 Corinthians 15:19)

We are already citizens of eternity bound for a heavenly reward that is wonderful beyond human comprehension. The LORD contrasts the two perspectives of life, one that is focused on time and the other that is focused on eternity, and gives their respective ends:

> **For, as I have often told you before and now say again even with tears, many live as enemies of the cross of Christ. Their destiny is destruction, their god is their stomach, and their glory is in their shame. Their mind is on EARTHLY THINGS. But our citizenship is in heaven. And we eagerly await a Savior from there, the Lord Jesus Christ, Who, by the power that enables Him to bring everything under His control, will transform our lowly bodies so that they will be like His glorious body.** (Philippians 3:18–21)

If we don't look at life through the perspective of eternity, then we will not cope well with time.

Many situations wouldn't make sense or seem fair if this life were all we had to look forward to. I will never forget experiencing just such a situation while speaking on the rapture (a time coming when the LORD Jesus will suddenly snatch us up to meet Him in the clouds and instantaneously transform our temporal bodies into bodies exactly like His). While giving the message, I noticed a portable hospital bed in the back with a nurse standing by.

After the lecture, I made my way to the rear of the hall to speak to the nurse and her patient. I found a young Vietnam veteran with no arms and no legs lying there. The nurse explained that he had trusted in Christ while she read to him a copy of *The Late Great Planet Earth*.[1] When I spoke to him, he asked me, "Hal, when Jesus transforms my body, will the new one have arms and legs?" I could hardly choke back the tears as I assured him that his new body would have perfect arms and legs. His eyes filled with hope as he smiled and said, "Oh praise the LORD. Now it isn't so bad."

One of the most inspiring and saintly persons I've ever met is Joni Eareckson Tada. She's been paralyzed from the neck down since she was a young teenager, yet her books have given hope and faith to so many people. Her condition would make no sense at all if it were divorced from the certainty of the rewards she will enjoy in eternal life.

Remember, **"Faith is being sure of what we hope for and certain of what we do not see."** When we have the certainty that every trial, every moment of suffering and sorrow, every deprivation in this life, which we endure through the power of the Holy Spirit, will be rewarded a thousandfold in eternity, then we can bear them with an inner joy, peace, and serenity that will sustain us through anything.

Each one of us will be touched by trials at one time or another and may ask, "Why did God allow this to happen to me?" Trying to understand the "why" of a trial is often one of the most painful parts of the trial itself. This is why I have searched the Scriptures for many years in an effort to discover what God says about trials. The following is a brief summary of what the Bible tells us concerning the reasons for suffering.

I. DISCIPLINE FOR SIN

One of the reasons there are trials and sufferings in the Christian's life is that they serve as a discipline for personal sin. The Bible says concerning the Christian's sin, **"Anyone, then, who knows the good he ought to do and doesn't do it, sins."** And also, **". . . everything that does not come from faith is sin."** (James 4:17 and Romans 14:23)

These two verses show that sin in the Christian's life is related to his present level of knowledge and faith. When we sin as a believer in one of these two ways, we break fellowship with the LORD. Sin does not sever our relationship, which is secured forever by the finished work of Christ on the cross, but it does break our fellowship. We remain out of fellowship until we confess our *known* sins to the LORD and begin to trust Him again (1 John 1:5–2:2).

If we fail to change our minds about sin and don't confess it, or if we keep choosing the same pattern of sin, then the LORD will discipline us in order to train us to walk with Him again.

This is what the Scripture says about discipline:

And you have forgotten that word of encouragement that addresses you as sons:

"My son, do not make light of the LORD's
      discipline,
and do not lose heart when He rebukes you,
because the LORD disciplines those He loves,
and He [corrects by scourging] everyone He
      accepts as a son."

Endure hardship as discipline; God is treating you as sons. For what son is not disciplined by his father? If you are not disciplined (and everyone undergoes discipline), then you are illegitimate children and not true sons.

Moreover, we have all had human fathers who disciplined us and we respected them for it. How much more should we submit to the Father of our spirits and live! Our fathers disciplined us for a little while as they thought best; but God disciplines us for our good, [for the purpose] that we may share in His holiness.

No discipline seems pleasant at the time, but painful. Later on, however, it produces a harvest of righteousness and peace for those who have been trained by it. (Hebrews 12:5–11)

I want to emphasize that this is only *one* of the reasons for trials in the Christian's life. Many Christians tend to think that this is the *only* reason for trials. This comes out of the great error of believing that all trials and suffering are direct retribution for some act of personal sin and unbelief. This has been a part of man's thinking from earliest records. Job's "three friends" reflected this as they debated about what kind of great

198

secret sin had brought such calamity upon him. But Job was not being disciplined because of some personal sin. The LORD Himself testified that Job was the most righteous man of his times.

The Discipline of Divine Love

It is whom the LORD *loves* that He disciplines. God loves us too much to let us waste our lives out of fellowship with Him, pursuing activities that will not only keep us miserable in this life, but empty-handed in eternity. From the moment we trust in Christ, we are saved forever. The Father could take us home right then, but He leaves us on this planet to share in His work of saving the lost, to train us for our eternal role as kings and priests with Christ, and to bring Him glory on earth. He gives us the precious opportunity to earn rewards that will be enjoyed for all eternity.

For this same reason, God sometimes withholds things from us that we want and feel we should have. As a teenager, I was not able to understand why my parents were so cruel and lacking in understanding as not to let me have a motorcycle. They were looking from a perspective that I was incapable of comprehending from my limited experience. A couple of years later, I did understand better, as I attended the funeral of a friend killed on a motorcycle. In a much greater way, The Heavenly Father looks at our lives from the vantage point of infinite wisdom and foreknowledge, guided by the desire to give us only the best.

Discipline versus Punishment

The LORD disciplines every child He receives because He loves him. But He doesn't punish a Christian in a harsh, punitive sense. All punishment of this sort due our sins was borne once and for all by the LORD Jesus on the cross. Discipline, on the other hand, is always forward looking and is designed to bring us back and keep us in fellowship with Christ. Punishment looks backward and repays an offender in proportion to the law he has broken.

If God ever paid us back for our sins, there would be nothing left of us. On this point, the Scripture says,

> **He does not treat us as our sins deserve**
> **or repay us according to our iniquities.**
> **For as high as the heavens are above the**
> **earth,**
> **so great is His love for those who fear**
> **[reverently trust] Him;**
> **as far as the east is from the west,**
> **so far has He removed our**
> **transgressions from us.** (Psalm 103:10–12)

Those who teach that God gets even with us for our sins love to use the following text to prove their point: **"Do not be deceived, God is not mocked; for whatever a man sows, this he will also reap."** (Galatians 6:7 NASB) This verse has been consistently misinterpreted by many ministers to apply to the principle of Divine discipline. If this were the correct interpretation, it would contradict everything the Bible teaches on the subject. It would mean that God punishes us for sin on the basis of the principle, "an eye for an eye and a tooth for a tooth." (This principle was given to judges of Israel for use in a civil law court and meant that they should make the punishment fit the crime.)

But when we put Galatians 6:7 into its context, it clearly speaks of the principle of supporting financially those who teach us God's word. The analogy of sowing and reaping is consistently used in connection with giving money to the LORD's work (compare 1 Corinthians 9:3–14 and 2 Corinthians 9:6–15 with Galatians 6:6–10). When these Scriptures are compared and kept in context, the meaning becomes obvious.

The consistent misinterpretation of Galatians 6 shows how prone Christians are to thinking of God as vengeful rather than loving and gracious. How it must grieve the heart of our loving Father, who did not spare His own Son in order to set Himself free to be gracious and merciful to us. We must beware of reading into the Bible a preconceived human bias that sees the LORD as anxiously awaiting the opportunity to get even with us for our sin.

Four Principles of Discipline

There are four main principles to remember about Divine discipline that will help us receive its training more quickly.

First, the *purpose* of discipline. **"God disciplines us for our good, that we may share in His holiness."** (Hebrews 12:10) Discipline is always for our benefit. The Father wants us to be truly happy and productive for eternity. His discipline is designed to teach us to live a holy life through the power of the Holy Spirit.

Second, discipline *is turned to blessing* as soon as we confess our sin and begin to believe God's promises again. The LORD's presence and comfort are immediately experienced when we believe the promises that God does not hold our sins against us (Psalm 130:3–5).

David writes of this aspect of discipline right after confessing his awful sins of murder, adultery, and deception. Note the progression of Psalm 32, which he wrote after he was back in fellowship with the LORD.

David's renewed appreciation of eternal security:

> **Blessed is he**
> **whose transgressions are forgiven,**
> **whose sins are covered.**
> **Blessed is the man**
> **whose sin the LORD does not count against**
> **him**
> **and in whose spirit is no deceit.**

David's remembrance of misery while out of fellowship:

> **When I kept silent [refusing to confess his sin],**
> **my bones wasted away**
> **through my groaning all day long.**

For day and night
Your hand was heavy upon me [in Divine
    discipline];
My strength was sapped
as in the heat of summer.

David's confession and immediate forgiveness:

> Then I acknowledged my sin to You
> and did not cover up my iniquity.
> I said, "I will confess
> my transgressions to the LORD"—
> and You forgave
> the guilt of my sin.

David's advice to those out of fellowship:

> Therefore let everyone who is godly pray
>   to You
> while You may be found [don't put off
>   confession of sin];
> surely when the mighty waters [of severe
>   discipline] rise,
> they will not reach him.

David's faith in God's promises:

> You are my hiding place;
> You will protect me from trouble
> and surround me with songs of deliverance
>   [and praise].

God's personal promise in response to David's faith:

> I WILL instruct you and teach you in the way
>   you should go;
> I WILL counsel you [with My eye upon] you.

David counsels us from his experience:

Do not be like the horse or the mule,
which have no understanding
but must be controlled . . .
or they will not come [near] you.

David's testimony of God's grace to those who believe:

Many are the woes of the wicked,
but the LORD's unfailing love
surrounds the man who trusts in Him.

God always responds to the faith of even the worst sinner. It is not primarily our sin that keeps us from being used by God, but our lack of faith. When we trust the LORD, He will keep us from sin through the power of the indwelling Holy Spirit. If the average Christian were to commit the sins that David did, it is doubtful he would have the faith to believe that God could use him again. The secret of David's continued usefulness to God after this terrible period of sin is his faith as expressed in the first two verses above. He believed that God was not holding his sin against him—and God wasn't.

Paul clearly speaks to the point:

In a large house there are articles not only of gold
and silver, but also of wood and clay; some are for
noble purposes and some for ignoble. If a man
cleanses himself from the latter, he will be an instru-
ment for noble purposes, made holy, useful to the
Master and prepared to do any good work.
(2 Timothy 2:20-21)

Isn't our Father wonderful? He is the God of another chance—not just a second chance, but another and another and another! How do we cleanse ourselves from sin? By claiming and believing 1 John 1:9!

Third, discipline is *temporary*. Once the LORD's discipline has taught us its intended lesson, it is either removed or turned into a blessing. On this point the Bible teaches: **"For His anger lasts only a moment, / but His favor lasts a lifetime; /**

weeping may remain for a night,/but rejoicing comes in the morning." (Psalm 30:5) And again, as Jeremiah wept over the discipline of Israel:

> Yet this I call to mind
> and therefore I have hope:
> [It is] because of the LORD's great love we
>   are not consumed,
> for His compassions never fail.
> They are new every morning;
> great is Your faithfulness. . . .
>
> Though He brings grief, He will show
>   compassion,
> so great is His unfailing love.
> For He does not willingly bring affliction
> or grief to the children of men.
>   (Lamentations 3:21–23, 32–33)

Fourth, there are *two possible results* of discipline. The result for the one who confesses his sin and trusts the LORD will be this: **"No discipline seems pleasant at the time, but painful. Later on, however, it produces a harvest of righteousness and peace for those who have been trained by it."** (Hebrews 12:11) So for this one, it produces a righteous behavior and an experience of God's peace.

The result for the one who does not trust the LORD's promises is expressed in this verse: **"See to it that no one misses the grace of God and that no [root of bitterness] grows up to cause trouble and defile many."** (Hebrews 12:15) If someone fails to believe in the grace of God, discipline will produce a root of bitterness that opens the door for Satan to enter his life. Then he will not only fall into greater sin, but cause many others to fall as well.

II. TRIALS TO KEEP US FROM PRIDE

The Scripture says that some trials are allowed into our lives to keep us from falling into pride. Pride was the original sin that caused Lucifer to fall and become Satan, and is the sin God says He hates above all others (see Proverbs 6:16–19). Because of this, the LORD takes special precautions to keep His servants from falling into this "snare of the Devil."

The sin of pride is a particular temptation for the servant of Christ who is given great spiritual gifts and understanding of God's Word. Listen to what the Apostle Paul shared concerning this:

> **To keep me from becoming conceited because of these surpassingly great revelations, there was given me a thorn in my flesh, a messenger of Satan, to torment me. Three times I pleaded with the LORD to take it away from me. But He said to me, "My grace is sufficient for you, for My power is made perfect in weakness." Therefore I will boast all the more gladly about my weaknesses, so that Christ's power may rest on me. That is why, for Christ's sake, I delight in weaknesses, in insults, in hardships, in persecutions, in difficulties. For when [I realize] I am weak, then I am [truly] strong.** (2 Corinthians 12:7–10)

There is some debate over what exactly Paul meant by the "thorn in his flesh." Whatever it was, it caused torment to Paul's body. Most careful Bible expositors believe that this was a very painful and troublesome eye disease, resulting from Paul's blinding vision of the LORD Jesus on the road to Damascus. Perhaps this chronic eye problem served as a constant reminder to Paul of how he was made blind so that he could see the truth.

The following passage indicates Paul's problem:

> **As you know, it was because of an illness that I first preached the gospel to you. Even though my illness was a trial to you, you did not treat me with contempt or scorn. . . . I can testify that, if you could have done so, you would have torn out your eyes and given them to me.** (Galatians 4:13–15)

We can draw the following conclusions from this passage:

First, the illness must have involved Paul's eyes or else the statement that the Galatians would have been willing, if possible, to give Paul their eyes would not make sense.

Second, the condition must have made Paul look so repulsive that it was a trial for them at first to receive him.

Third, God used this flare-up of Paul's eye disease to force him to stay long enough in Galatia to preach the gospel to them.

Fourth, this should answer the inaccurate contention on the part of some that say God *never* allows sickness into the life of a Christian who is believing Him and walking with Him. God used Paul's illness to guide him into evangelizing the vast region of Galatia, which he apparently would otherwise have bypassed. I believe that God desires to heal most of us, but there are some special cases, as illustrated here, where He has a greater purpose to accomplish. And in these cases, you can pray until you're blue in the face and there will be no healing. We must seek the LORD's will in all our prayers, not merely our own. But of this we can be certain: If a person who is ill has confessed every known sin in his life, and if the LORD does not immediately heal him, then the LORD in His love and wisdom has a greater purpose that perhaps *we* may not understand in this life, but that will certainly count for all eternity.

God used this eye illness (and possibly other physical afflictions) not only to keep Paul from pride, but to keep him aware of the weakness and inadequacy of human ability to accomplish His work. This caused Paul to depend constantly on the Holy Spirit to fill and empower his life, so that he was truly strong.

Paul pleaded with the LORD in three specific prayer sessions to take the disease away, but the LORD clearly showed him the greater purpose in it. After that, Paul not only accepted the bodily affliction, but embraced it as God's will.

We may be missing a greater blessing in an affliction simply because we refuse to accept God's purpose in it. Rather than learning how to be strong through realizing our weakness as Paul did, we often, like spoiled children, demand an instant removal of all affliction.

III. TRIALS TO BUILD FAITH

The experiences of the Exodus generation are among God's greatest historical lessons for teaching us how He uses trials to make us crack the faith barrier.

Peter spoke of this purpose for trials when he said,

In this [salvation] you greatly rejoice; even though now for a little while, if necessary, you have been distressed by various trials, [for the purpose] that the proof of your FAITH, being more precious than gold which is perishable, even though tested by fire, may be found to result in praise and glory and honor at the revelation of Jesus Christ. (1 Peter 1:6–7 NASB)

The Greek word *dokimé*, which is translated "proof," means something put to the test for the purpose of proving its genuineness. The comparison of the proving of faith to gold being purified by fire gives a graphic illustration. Gold is purified when it is heated over fire. This causes all the impurities to come to the top so that they can easily be raked off. The believer's faith is purified when trials cause his impurities to be cast aside.

Just examine the lives of all the men of the Bible who served God in a mighty way. Moses, David, Job, Daniel, and the apostles, to name a few. All of these men had their faith tried and proven by fire.

Paul the apostle singlehandedly took the Gospel of Christ to the outer limits of the Roman Empire in his lifetime. And he did this without any means of modern transportation or communication. No one has equaled that performance since. Yet listen to what the LORD told Paul when He called him: **"But the LORD [told] Ananias, 'Go! This man is My chosen instrument to carry My name before the Gentiles and their kings and before the people of Israel. I WILL SHOW HIM HOW MUCH HE MUST SUFFER FOR MY NAME.'"** (Acts 9:15–16) How is that for a positive confession? The LORD

didn't give Paul much with which to develop a positive attitude. Perhaps some modern teachers would say that the LORD
needed a little crash course in "positive thinking" here.

As I said before, faith is like a muscle. Just as muscle tis-
sue gets flabby through lack of exercise, so faith gets flabby
through lack of challenge. A person can develop faith through
learning from the trials of the biblical heroes of faith. But quan-
tum leaps of faith are usually learned by personal experience.

IV. TRIALS THAT CAUSE GROWTH

James, the half brother of the LORD Jesus, comments on
this: **"Consider it all joy, my brethren, when you encounter
various trials, knowing that the testing of your faith produces
endurance** [faith in the long run]. **And let endurance have its
perfect result, that you may be [MATURE] and complete,
lacking in nothing."** (James 1:2–4 NASB) Here, various trials
produce a special kind of faith, which brings about overall
spiritual maturity. This special faith is called endurance, which
is a faith that persists and doesn't give up when deliverance is
delayed. The Bible likens the Christian life to running a race:
**". . . let us run with endurance the race that is set before us,
fixing our eyes on Jesus, the author and perfecter of [our]
faith."** (Hebrews 12:1–2 NASB) The idea is that God wants distance runners, not sprinters, in this race of living by faith.
Some Christians are like sprinters: they believe the LORD for a
short while in a quick burst of faith—and then fall apart. God
wants those who keep on believing and waiting upon Him
even though the trials persist. This develops true maturity.

Paul also commented on the trials that bring about maturity:

> **Not only so, but we also rejoice in our sufferings,
> because we know that suffering produces persever-
> ance; perseverance, [proven] character; and [proven]
> character, hope. And hope does not disappoint us,
> because God has poured out His love into our hearts
> by the Holy Spirit, whom He has given us.** (Romans
> 5:3–5)

It isn't that God is trying to produce a bunch of spiritual masochists, but rather that for a limited time, certain trials are necessary to produce growth and proven character. But the LORD reminds us that His love is made particularly manifest to us by the Holy Spirit during these times.

V. TRIALS THAT TEACH OBEDIENCE AND DISCIPLINE

All the biblical heroes of faith who were used significantly first went through a period of testing and training.

As we analyze some of God's greatest servants, we discover that all went through tests and trials not because of some personal sin, but because God wanted to strengthen their personal discipline so that they could stand in the face of Satan's attacks.

The greatest example is the LORD Jesus Christ Himself. The writer to the Hebrews spoke of this:

In the days of His life on earth, He offered up both prayers and supplications with loud crying and tears to the One able to deliver Him out of death, and He was heard because of His humble submission [namely, He was resurrected]. **Although He was a Son He learned obedience from the things which He suffered.** (Hebrews 5:7-8 HL)

Jesus, the Son of God, is the most unique person in the universe. He is both absolute God and true humanity forever united in one person. It is in His true human nature that He was trained in obedience and discipline. As soon as Jesus started His public ministry, His discipline of faith and obedience to the Father were severely tested by the Devil (see Luke 4:1-8).

Paul is another example. The Lord Jesus' command to Ananias when he was sent to speak to Paul (who was then known as the dangerous Saul of Tarsus) was, **"'Go, for he is a chosen instrument of Mine, to bear My name before the Gentiles and kings and the sons of Israel; for I will show him how much he must suffer for My name's sake.'"** (Acts 9:15–16 NASB) This is not the way the world would recruit one of its chief leaders, is it? The problem is, both Christians and those in the world fail to realize that it is possible to be content and full of joy even in the midst of trials. This is the testimony that Paul later gave:

> **But I rejoiced in the LORD greatly. Not that I speak from want; for I have learned to be content in whatever circumstances I am. I know how to get along with humble means, and I also know how to live in prosperity; in any and every circumstance I have learned the secret of being filled and going hungry, both of having abundance and suffering need. I can do all things through Christ who keeps on strengthening me.** (Philippians 4:11–13 HL)

Not everyone will go through this kind of trial. Still, there is a principle involved: the greater the mission, the greater the need for training in obedience and discipline. This is why Jesus cautioned those who wanted to follow Him as *leaders* to first count the cost.

VI. TRIALS THAT PREVENT US FROM FALLING INTO SIN

The heavenly Father knows that we have certain areas of weakness that make us vulnerable to particular temptations. So sometimes, He allows trials into our lives to prevent us from falling into sin.

Peter comments on this: **"Therefore, since Christ has suffered in the flesh, arm yourselves also with the same purpose, because he who has suffered in the flesh has ceased from sin, so as to live the rest of the time in the flesh no longer for the lusts of men, but for the will of God."** (1 Peter 4:1–2 NASB)

Suffering directed by the loving hand of God prevents us from being susceptible to our areas of weakness. Suffering also encourages us to pursue God's will for our lives, because it takes our mind off the trivial things of this life and focuses it on the things of God.

I have discipled so many super-talented young men who would have been drawn astray by the things of this world if the LORD had not gotten their attention through trials. God also broke the hold that certain areas of sin had upon some, by putting them through purifying trials.

Just as Paul was kept from falling into pride through a painful affliction, so suffering keeps us back from the areas of weakness in our old sin nature.

VII. TRIALS THAT EQUIP US TO COMFORT OTHERS

Some trials give us the capacity to empathize with others who are in a similar situation.

Blessed be the God and Father of our Lord Jesus Christ, the Father of mercies and God of all comfort; Who comforts us in all our affliction SO THAT we may be able to comfort those who are in any affliction with the comfort with which we ourselves are comforted by God. (2 Corinthians 1:3-4 NASB)

Let's take one example: There is no one who can comfort someone who has lost a loved one as well as a person who has been comforted by the LORD in the same experience. This person can share with such conviction and power how God comforted him in his sorrow that he will inspire faith and comfort.

Those who have great ministries of counseling and showing mercy usually have had a number of personal trials. This gives them an insight, understanding, and empathy that can be gained in no other way.

VIII. TRIALS THAT PROVE THE REALITY OF CHRIST IN US

The supernatural life of Christ lived out through a Christian is most manifest when through faith he undergoes trials with an attitude of praise and a radiant face stemming from inner joy. This is so contrary to normal human behavior that the unbeliever is confronted with the Christ we proclaim.

Paul frequently taught about this in the autobiographical sections of his writings. He spoke of the Holy Spirit's ministry of living the life of Christ through us: **"But we have this treasure in earthen vessels, that the surpassing greatness of the power may be** [demonstrated to be] **of God and not from ourselves."** (2 Corinthians 4:7 NASB) Then Paul writes of how this treasure of Christ's life in him was lived out in his experiences:

> **We are hard pressed on every side, but not crushed; perplexed, but not in despair; persecuted, but not abandoned; struck down, but not destroyed. We always carry around in our body the death of Jesus, SO THAT THE LIFE OF JESUS MAY ALSO BE REVEALED IN OUR BODY. For we who are alive are always being given over to death for Jesus' sake, SO THAT HIS LIFE MAY BE REVEALED IN OUR MORTAL BODY.** (2 Corinthians 4:8–11)

Paul's point is that Christ's life is revealed to the world through our supernatural response to our trials and tribulations.

IX. TRIALS THAT GLORIFY GOD

There are many examples of this kind of trial. One that inspires me most is the case of the three young Hebrew men named Shadrach, Meshach, and Abednego. In a day when most of the Hebrews taken as prisoners to Babylon after the destruction of Jerusalem were compromising their faith in the LORD, these three brought great glory to God by the tenacity and boldness of their faith in the face of a horrible death.

King Nebuchadnezzar built a ninety-foot-tall idol of gold and decreed that when the royal band played, all would be required to fall down and worship it. Those disobedient would be thrown into a great blazing furnace.

Some jealous court astrologers reported to the king that certain Jews he had appointed over his affairs of state refused to bow down and worship the idol. In a furious rage, Nebuchadnezzar called the three young Jews in and asked them if in fact they had refused to worship his idol.

Observe their bold faith in their reply:

"O Nebuchadnezzar, we do not need to defend ourselves before you in this matter. If we are thrown into the blazing furnace, the God we serve is able to save us from it, and He will rescue us from your hand, O king. But even if He does not, we want you to know, O king, that we will not serve your gods or worship the image of gold you have set up." (Daniel 3:16–18)

The king, infuriated by their answer, ordered the great blazing furnace heated seven times hotter than ever before.

So Shadrach, Meshach, and Abednego, securely bound, were thrown into the great furnace. The flames were so intense that the men who carried out the sentence were killed by the heat. It was at this point that the young Jews' faith brought great glory to God. The Scripture reports:

Then King Nebuchadnezzar leaped to his feet in amazement and asked his advisers, "[Wasn't it] three men that we tied up and threw into the fire?" They replied, "Certainly, O king." He said, "Look! I see four men walking around in the fire unbound and unharmed, and the fourth looks like a son of the gods." (Daniel 3:24–25)

What a picture this paints! The only thing that we lose in our God-given trials are the things that bind us. And the Son of God makes Himself especially near and intimate during these times.

This so impressed the king that he not only promoted these three young men of faith, but also passed a decree that no one could speak evil of their God on pain of death.

Our God has not changed. The LORD will still perform mighty miracles for His glory's sake and to reveal Himself, as He sovereignly wishes.

All the martyrs of the faith, such as Stephen, brought glory to God through this kind of trial. God didn't miraculously save the martyrs as he did Shadrach, Meshach, and Abednego, but their white robes will shine as a brilliant testimony of their faith for all eternity to witness.

X. TRIALS FOR A TESTIMONY TO THE ANGELS

The book of Job takes us behind the scenes in heaven and reveals an awesome conflict that exists there between God and His angels, and Satan and his demons.

The Scriptures reveal: **"One day the angels came to present themselves before the LORD, and Satan also came with them. The LORD said to Satan, 'Where have you come from?'**

"Satan answered the LORD, 'from roaming through the earth and going back and forth in it.'" (Job 1:6–7)

This was an insolent answer in which Satan boasted to God of his ownership of the earth. As noted before, Adam betrayed God by forfeiting the title deed of the earth to Satan.

In reply, God challenged Satan, saying there was one man on earth that he didn't own. The LORD said to Satan, **"'Have you considered My servant Job? There is no one on earth like him; he is blameless and upright, a man who fears God and shuns evil.'"** (Job 1:8)

Satan told the LORD that the only reason Job followed Him was because He had protected and blessed him so much. Satan challenged God: **"'Stretch out Your hand and strike everything he has, and he will surely curse You to Your face.'"** (Job 1:11)

The LORD accepted the challenge and gave Satan permission to destroy everything that Job had without touching Job himself. This Satan did with a vengeance. He destroyed all of his possessions and killed all of his children. He then timed the news of all these disasters so that several reports came in one after another. This gave maximum impact to the horrible news.

Job continued to trust in the LORD even though the tests got so severe he was driven almost out of his mind. Later the LORD restored all that he had lost manyfold.

The main purpose of the book of Job is to show that God's judgment of Satan and his angels was just. Job, compared to the angels was a vastly inferior creature in intelligence and knowledge of God, yet he chose to believe in and follow the

LORD despite tremendous adversity. This demonstrates that Satan, with his superior attributes and a full intimate knowledge of God, had no excuse for rebelling against Him.

God's Revelation to the Angels

Many times trials of a lesser degree are allowed into the life of a believer in order to demonstrate further this same point. Angels continue to observe constantly the acts of human faith. Every aspect of God's dealing with mankind is teaching the angelic realm more about the wonder of God's infinite character.

The Apostle Paul spoke of this when he explained the purpose of his ministry and the wonder of God's grace:

> **Although I am less than the least of all God's people, this grace was given me: to preach to the Gentiles the unsearchable riches of Christ, and to make plain to everyone the administration of this mystery, which for ages past was kept hidden in God, who created all things. His intent was that now, through the church, the manifold wisdom of God should be made known to the rulers and authorities in the heavenly realms** [high ranking officials of the angels]**, according to His eternal purpose which He accomplished in Christ Jesus our Lord.** (Ephesians 3:8–11)

According to this, God is teaching the angels about His manifold wisdom, particularly through His dealings with the Church. Before "Operation Man," there was no occasion for angels to see God's attributes of love, justice, and wisdom fully demonstrated. But with the creation of man and his consequent rebellion, these attributes of God's character have been fully demonstrated. Above all, the infinite beauty and wonder of God's grace has been revealed to both the unfallen and fallen angels.

IN DEFENSE OF JOB

A few ministers today teach that the reason Job suffered such trials was because of his "negative confession" when he said, **"What I feared has come upon me;/what I dreaded has happened to me."** (Job 3:25) I believe God will make these men apologize to Job when they get to heaven. To make a statement like this is to demonstrate a complete lack of understanding of the purpose of the book of Job.

God holds up Job as one of the Bible's supreme models of persevering faith in the following Scriptures:

> **"As surely as I live, declares the Sovereign LORD, even if Noah, Daniel and Job were in it** [a country consigned to Divine judgment], **they could save neither son nor daughter. They would save only themselves by their righteousness."** (Ezekiel 14:20)

> **Brothers, as an example of patience in the face of suffering, take the prophets who spoke in the name of the LORD. As you know, we consider blessed those who have persevered. You have heard of Job's perseverance and have seen what the LORD finally brought about. The LORD is full of compassion and mercy.** (James 5:10–11)

The LORD doesn't applaud a man's faith in this way if the reason for his trials was discipline for a "negative confession." Some teachers strive so hard to make their preconceived doctrines fit the Scriptures that they twist all those verses that don't quite fit their view.

Very few, if any, will ever be called upon to suffer trials as severe as Job's, but angels learn from every situation where humans choose to believe God in the midst of trials.

Jesus' Negative Confession

Given the assumptions of the "Positive Confession" teachers, even Jesus could be accused of "negative confession." Listen to what He said:

216

From that time on Jesus began to explain to His disciples that He must go up to Jerusalem and suffer many things at the hands of the elders, chief priests and teachers of the law, and that He must be killed and on the third day be raised to life. (Matthew 16:21)

Peter didn't like this at all. He was the original "positive confessor." He actually *rebuked* Jesus and told Him that this would never happen to Him. (Matthew 16:22) To Peter, this was a negative, defeatist confession. It didn't fit in with *his* ambition of being a ruler in God's kingdom, or his expectation that this would happen very soon.

Listen to what some of the "Positive Confession" teachers say, and then try to reconcile their teachings with Jesus' statement. One popular advocate of this doctrine taught, "If you confess sickness, it will develop sickness within your system. If you talk about your doubts and fears, they will become stronger. If you confess the lack of finances, it will stop the money from coming in."

Another famous advocate of "Positive Confession" wrote, ". . . All our words should be words of faith. We are to say only words that we want to come to pass and believe that they all will produce results. By getting into the Word of God and continually feeding on the Word so that faith controls your vocabulary, you can come to the place where all your words will come to pass." (These two statements are representative of what the "Positive Confession" movement generally believes.)

If this teaching is true, then Jesus created His own arrest, physical abuse and crucifixion by His "negative confession."

As we examine this teaching, however, an important question to ask is this, Who determines what is positive and/or good for our lives? Most of us would always choose a prosperous, trouble-free life that is free from any semblance of suffering and deprivation. So our "positive confessions" generally reflect that human viewpoint. We demand that God immediately deliver us from all difficulties and suffering. We claim "our rights to wealth and prosperity." But the Bible reveals that the most important thing to consider in each one of life's circumstances is God's will. I believe in a positive confession of my faith in God's promises. But I also know that there is nothing magical about mouthing words. Nothing that pleases God will result unless I have a confidence of God's will and an understanding of why God keeps His Word. The more I know about God Himself, His faithfulness, love and power, the more I will trust in His promises.

The way Jesus answered Peter's objection to His prediction of His imminent arrest, torture, and execution is the way He would answer much of what is being practiced in the "Positive Confession" movement today:

Jesus turned and said to Peter, "Out of my sight Satan! You are a stumbling block to me; you do not have in mind the things of God, but the things of men." (Matthew 16:23)

This reflects the main flaw I have observed in the "Positive Confession" teachings. In many cases they demand the "things of men, not the things of God." Peter wanted a *crown* without a *cross*. Satan even tempted Jesus to take a crown without a cross. (Luke 4:1–8) This is one of his favorite tactics. The Bible presents a very different expectation of life than these "Positive Confessors" generally teach. The Scriptures teach:

But how is it to your credit if you receive a beating for doing wrong and endure it? But if you suffer for doing good and you endure it, this is commendable before God. To this you were called, because Christ suffered for you, leaving you an example, that you should follow in his steps. (1 Peter 2:20–21)

THE TWELFTH COMMANDMENT

Let me emphasize again that God will never allow you to be tested above what you are able to stand. The LORD intends for us to enter His rest in whatever circumstance we find ourselves. As we saw through the study of God's dealing with the Exodus generation, this is possible through believing His promises.

Whether we are going through a trial, or experiencing a period of trouble-free abundance, the LORD wants us to remember His "twelfth commandment," *Thou shalt not sweat it!*

(The eleventh commandment is "love others as I have loved you.")

Because of our hope for eternity, our sustenance and empowerment through the indwelling Holy Spirit, and the promises of God for our every need, we can experience what God through James commands: **"Consider it pure joy, my brothers, whenever you face trials of many kinds, because you know that the testing of your faith develops perseverance. Perseverance must finish its work so that you may be mature and complete, not lacking anything."** (James 1:2–4)

CHAPTER SEVENTEEN

Endurance in the Race of Faith

Therefore, since we are surrounded by such a great cloud of witnesses, let us throw off everything that hinders and the sin that so easily entangles us, and let us keep running with endurance the race that is marked out for us. Let us look away from all that would distract and fix our eyes on JESUS, the author and perfecter of our faith, who for the sake of the joy set before Him endured the cross, scorning its shame, and sat down at the right hand of God. Keep your mind dwelling upon Him who endured such opposition from sinful men, so that you will not grow weary and lose heart.

Hebrews 12:1–3 HL

THE DYNAMICS OF WAITING ON THE LORD

One of life's most difficult things is to keep on trusting the LORD when He delays answering our faith. Yet this is one of the most necessary aspects of a test designed to develop combat faith.

As the Scripture quoted above indicates, our heavenly Father wants to develop distance runners, not sprinters, in the race of faith He has marked out for each one of us. A sprinter puts on a short burst of speed and then he is finished. A marathon runner is characterized above all by tenacity, perseverance, and endurance. He keeps on running when every muscle cries stop. In the same way, the LORD wants us to run the spiritual race of life with an endurance that perseveres in spite of delays, obstacles, misunderstandings, and discouragements.

I have sought to help many believers crack the faith barrier and press on to combat faith, but the most common problem has been "losing heart" and giving up because the LORD delayed in delivering them out of a trial. Like a sprinter, they put on "a burst of faith" in the promises of God, but were soon discouraged when the LORD did not immediately deliver them.

The opening verses of this chapter teach essential lessons in the development of combat faith. These verses come at the climax of God's Hall of Fame for the heroes of faith in Hebrews 11. This passage presents the LORD Jesus as the supreme example of faith that perseveres under trial, which I have called combat faith.

LEARNING TO RUN IN GOD'S RACE

We are reminded by the writer to the Hebrews of the great cloud of witnesses who are the heroes of faith now in heaven. Their example was written in God's word to encourage our faith and show us the way of entering God's rest.

Using the analogy of the ancient Olympic distance races, the writer gives us some vital training instructions for living the life of faith.

Casting Off Excess Baggage

No distance runner carries any excess weight along. This is what is meant by **"let us throw off everything that hinders."** We may be called upon to get rid of some habits and relationships in our lives that could weigh us down. If we make a choice to be used of God, there are some things that must be laid aside through the power of the Holy Spirit. If something is a hindrance to God's will in your life, the Holy Spirit will reveal it to you. Then as you depend upon Him, He will empower you to cast it aside.

All of us have certain areas of weakness in our old sin nature that are particularly vulnerable to temptation. This is what is meant by **"the sin that so easily entangles us."** The Holy Spirit is the only one that can deal with these areas of weakness. But when we walk by a faith-dependence upon Him, He gives us victory over temptation and keeps us from being thrown off stride and tripped up.

Endurance: the Essence of Combat Faith

We are commanded to **"keep running with endurance the race marked out for us."** The root of the Greek term μόνη means *to abide*. With the preposition ὑπο added, it literally means "to dwell or endure under a burden." It came to mean "endurance, perseverance, or patience under stress." This paints a graphic picture of persevering in faith under trial.

I can remember a few times when I was so numb and in shock as a result of a trial that I could hardly think. I could only point to a promise in my Bible, look up to God, and say, "I believe and claim this, Father, now strengthen me and don't let me fall apart." It took a moment-by-moment focusing of my faith on the promises to keep me from fainting in my mind and giving up. But, do you know something, the LORD has never let me down. He has always strengthened me when I trusted Him to do so. Through many tough experiences, I began to learn the dynamics of waiting on the LORD.

One of the key passages that teach about waiting on the LORD was revealed by Isaiah:

Do you not know? Have you not heard?
The Everlasting God, the LORD, the Creator of
the ends of the earth
does not become weary or tired.
His understanding is inscrutable.
He gives STRENGTH to the weary,

and to the one who lacks might He increases
   POWER.
Even though youths grow weary and tired,
and the athletes stumble badly,
yet those who KEEP WAITING upon the LORD
will EXCHANGE THEIR STRENGTH;
they will mount up with wings like eagles,
they will keep on running and not grow weary,
they will continue walking and not faint.
   (Isaiah 40:28–31 HL)

This beautiful promise has sustained me through many trials. It begins by reminding us that God never gets tired or lacks power for any purpose. It also reminds us that He understands every detail of our life. Then it promises that those who **"wait upon the LORD will EXCHANGE their strength."** The Hebrew word that is translated as "renew" in most Bibles literally means "to exchange one thing for another." When the way is so tough that even young men and athletes are falling, God promises that He will exchange His almighty strength for our human strength. The only qualification is that we "keep on waiting upon the LORD." The term "to wait" here means "to persevere in trusting the LORD under extreme stress." It is a word for "faith that perseveres."

Another promise that has sustained me in the roughest times is this:

"You will keep in perfect peace
the one whose mind is focused upon You,
because he trusts in You.
Trust in the LORD forever,
for in the LORD Jehovah
is everlasting strength."
   (Isaiah 26:3–4 HL)

Again this stresses a tenacious focusing of the mind upon the LORD and His faithfulness. I have claimed this promise so many times in the midst of trials and experienced the miracle of the peace of God that surpasses all understanding.

It is a matter of trusting in the LORD with a marathon

faith, not a sprinting faith. It means to keep on believing in God's promise when all human hope is gone—when the only hope you have is the knowledge that God must be faithful to keep His promises. We can build our confidence upon the fact that He simply cannot lie. He must keep His Word when we believe it. The greater the odds against us, the more God is pleased with our faith.

The great former basketball coach of UCLA, Johnny Wooden, used to say, "When the going gets tough, the tough get going." I like that. Only we might put it this way: "When the going gets tough, the tough keep believing."

The LORD has a specific plan for everyone's life. This is what is meant by **"the race marked out for us."** We are not in competition with anyone but ourselves. We are competing with the course marked out for us, striving to achieve the maximum within the perimeters of God's personal plan for us.

JESUS, THE SUPREME EXAMPLE OF COMBAT FAITH

Two commands are given to us at the beginning of verses two and three. Both show that focusing upon the way Jesus lived as a man in this world is the key to victory.

This first command is literally, **"Let us keep looking away from all that distracts and fix our eyes on Jesus."** The Greek verb, ἀφορῶντες which is translated "fixing our eyes on" in the NASB, really means much more. It is a present participle, which emphasizes that it is to be a continuous action. The verb not only means to "fix our eyes on Jesus," but also "to look away from all that would distract us from concentrating on Him." I used to be a sprinter and I can still remember losing an important race because I took my eyes off the finish line and glanced back at my competition. In running, you have to concentrate on the finish line and keep driving toward it. Similarly, we must totally focus our eye of faith upon Jesus to win the race of God's calling for our life.

We have to keep our eyes fixed upon Jesus and his example. He is not only the author of living by faith, He also stepped out of eternity into time and lived His own plan. In other words, He is not a coach who sits in the stands. He came down into our arena and perfectly demonstrated how His faith plan worked.

Remember, in His human nature, Jesus had to depend upon the Holy Spirit the same way we do. Thus He left us the supreme example of living by faith. He is the perfecter of the life of faith. The same Holy Spirit that lived that incredible life through Jesus now dwells in you and me—and He has lost none of His power. This is what we are to fix our eyes upon. We have the same means of living the Christian life as Jesus did!

We are to meditate upon the fact that Jesus fixed His eyes upon the goal, which was the joy of saving forever all of us who would receive the pardon purchased by His sacrificial death. He endured the cross because of the joy our salvation would bring Him.

The second command is to **"focus your mind upon Him."** As we keep considering the trials that Jesus endured, and remember that we have the same means of enduring as He did, we are encouraged and our faith is strengthened.

WHEN DELIVERANCE IS DELAYED

When deliverance is delayed, keep on trusting the LORD. When His purpose is finished, He will deliver you no matter how much of a miracle is required.

Believe this promise and our God and Father will sustain you:

> **Be self-controlled and alert. Your enemy the devil prowls around like a roaring lion looking for someone to devour. Resist him, standing firm in the faith, because you know that your brothers throughout the world are undergoing the same kind of sufferings.**
>
> **And the God of all grace, who called you to His eternal glory in Christ, after you have suffered a little while, will Himself restore you and make you strong, firm and steadfast.** (1 Peter 5:8–10)

And remember,

. . . They that keep waiting upon the LORD
will exchange their strength
[**for His,** strength through the Holy Spirit within us];
they will mount up with wings as eagles,
they will keep running and not get tired,
they will keep walking and not become weary.
    (Isaiah 40:31 HL)

"Behold, I am the Lord,
the God of all flesh;
is anything too difficult for Me?"
    (Jeremiah 32:27 NASB)

CHAPTER EIGHTEEN

Focusing on Things Not Seen

Now we see but a poor reflection . . . ; then we shall see face to face. Now I know in part; then I shall know fully, even as I am fully known . . . .

**"No eye has seen,
no ear has heard,
no mind has conceived
what God has prepared for those who love Him."**
1 Corinthians 13:12 and 2:9

It is exciting to know that every decision, every act of obedience, every act of faith, every trial endured, will have eternal repercussions. Everything we do in this life is significant and can earn us eternal rewards. Nothing is without meaning.

In a very real sense, this life is a kind of training for the next. We are being prepared for an eternal mission in our Heavenly Father's infinite universe. The way we respond to our opportunities to believe the LORD now, qualifies us for our future position and role in His kingdom. Jesus hinted at this when in a parable he said that those who have been faithful in ten things will be made ruler over ten cities, and those who have been faithful in five things will be made ruler over five cities (Luke 19:11–27).

The rewards we'll get in the future are of a magnitude so much greater than the tiny dimensions of our faithful services in the present that they defy human comprehension. It's as if we will be given a twenty-carat flawless diamond for a grain of sand.

Just note the superlatives God uses in comparing our present labors with our future rewards and glory: **"For momentary, light affliction is producing for us an eternal weight [measure] of glory far beyond all comparison, while we look not at the things which are seen, . . . for the things which are seen are temporal, but the things which are not seen are eternal."** (2 Corinthians 4:17–18 NASB)

From the beginning of this book I've stressed God's definition of faith. It is **"being sure of what we HOPE for and CERTAIN of what we do not see."** The Spirit of God caused the Apostle Paul to share his own experiences often, because they give us a model of living by faith. As he stresses in the Scripture, the considerable trials he endured for the sake of the Gospel were in his estimation only light, momentary afflictions not worthy of being compared with the eternal measure of glory with which Christ will reward him.

Paul declared that he could have such an attitude because he **"LOOKED at the things not seen."** The word translated as **"look"** is a present tense participle that literally means **"to keep your eye focused upon the things not seen."** Isn't it fascinating that Paul kept focusing on things that are not visible? This must mean that he focused with his "eye of faith" upon the unseen world of the future that God has promised.

This is the secret of endurance in our battles of faith and the way to win the victory. Jesus has already won the war. By trusting and resting in Him, we enter His victory in our battles.

There is never any need to lose heart or be discouraged, because though our physical body deteriorates with age, our inner spiritual self is being renewed day by day. As I approach sixty years of age, and my once trim and muscular body begins to decline in spite of all my efforts to eat right and exercise regularly, it's such a comfort to see my spirit growing stronger. It's also wonderful to know that the "worst" thing I have to look forward to is this body dying and my spirit going instantly to be consciously present with the LORD (2 Corinthians 5:6–8). Hallelujah!

Let's take an inventory of the **"unseen things"** promised for the future, so that we will be able to focus constantly our eye of faith upon them.

THE ETERNAL THINGS THAT ARE NOT SEEN

The details of our coming eternal life with God are not fully revealed. Apparently we just wouldn't be able to take it all in. But enough is revealed to challenge and encourage our faith through the darkest and most difficult moments of this life. Once again, the LORD makes us this beautiful promise: **"Things which eye has not seen and ear has not heard,/and which have not entered the heart of man,/All that God has prepared for those who love Him."** (1 Corinthians 2:9 NASB)

Our New Bodies

Though this body is wearing out, and we sometimes groan with aging, pain, and injuries, we are going to get a new one that is perfect, eternal, and just like Jesus' resurrected body. He is going to instantaneously transform these temporal bodies into a new form.

It appears that our new bodies will be able to travel by thought and walk through solid materials. They will never wear out, experience sickness, pain, aging, or corruption. We don't have to eat, but we can if we choose to—and not get fat!

Our bodies will reflect the glory of God. They will be designed for the spiritual nature and sphere, and will be suitable for the very presence of God. Though greatly beautified, we will be able to recognize each other. (PTL) (1 Corinthians 15 and Philippians 3:20–21)

Our New Dwelling Place

The center of God's new universe will be the New Jerusalem. It will be a city of dazzling beauty made of every kind of precious stone and metal. God Himself will dwell there and the light of His glory will eliminate night and darkness forever (Revelation 21 and 22).

The LORD Jesus' throne will also be there, and those who have persevered in trials will sit upon His throne with Him (Revelation 3:21).

There will be no more curse upon the earth or the heavens. Nature will be returned to its original pre-sin perfection. I love to visit and gaze upon certain places like Switzerland, where the mountains, rivers, and forests are so naturally beautiful. But just think, if some of these places are so pretty now, what will they be without a curse on them?

Although our principal dwelling place will be the New Jerusalem, we will apparently be able to observe the rest of the universe, since we will be kings and priests with Christ over all God's domain.

OUR CROWNS

There are certain crowns promised as special rewards for service.

The Crown of Righteousness

"I have finished the race, I have kept the faith. Now there is in store for me the CROWN OF RIGHTEOUSNESS, which the LORD, the righteous Judge, will award to me on that day—and not only to me, but also to all who have longed for his appearing." (2 Timothy 4:7-8)

This is a reward for those who have taken literally the prophecy about the potential of the LORD Jesus Christ's any-moment manifestation in the Rapture. The verb translated as **"have longed"** is literally *"to love"* in the perfect tense. This speaks of one who has intensely longed or yearned for the LORD's sudden coming for the Church in the Rapture.

This also includes the idea contained in 1 John 3:2-3, which says, **"Dear friends, now we are children of God, and what we will be has not yet been made known. But we know that when He appears, we shall be like Him, for we shall see**

Him as He is. Everyone who has this hope in him PURIFIES himself, just as He is pure." No one can consistently long for the possibility of the LORD's any-moment appearance and not seek to live his life in such a way as to be unashamed when it happens. All those who long for His appearance will receive this crown.

The Crown of Life

Blessed is the man who perseveres under trial, because when he has stood the test, he will receive the CROWN OF LIFE that God has promised to those who love Him. (James 1:12)

"Do not be afraid of what you are about to suffer. I tell you, the devil will put some of you in prison to test you, and you will suffer persecution for ten days Be faithful, even to the point of death, and I will give you the CROWN OF LIFE." (Revelation 2:10)

This reward is both for the martyrs and those who have persevered under special trials for the LORD's sake. Whether we are faithful in our trials to the point of a martyr's death, or we persevere in faith under trials while the LORD, for His own reasons, delays deliverance, we will receive this very special crown with much honor and glory.

When Stephen, the Church's first martyr, stood before the religious leaders of Israel to prove to them from their own Scriptures that they had murdered their own Messiah, his face glowed with the glory of God and appeared as the face of an angel (Acts 6:15). Stephen knew that he was signing his own death warrant, yet by faith, filled with the irresistible power of the Holy Spirit, he pressed home a witness that they could not refute or resist.

When the leaders could not stand the truth of what they heard, they stopped their ears and rushed upon Stephen like a pack of savage wolves. They brutally dragged him out of a city gate and stoned him to death. But Stephen saw into heaven as he was dying and gave us a foretaste of the honor our LORD will give to those who receive this crown. This is the account of Stephen's last moments: **"But Stephen, full of the Holy Spirit, looked up to heaven and saw the glory of God, and JESUS STANDING at the right hand of God. 'Look,' he said, 'I see heaven open and the Son of Man standing at the right hand of God.'"** (Acts 7:55–56) The Scriptures say that Jesus *sits* at the right hand of God. But our LORD, the Sovereign of the universe, rose to his feet to welcome into His presence this faithful witness, and to place upon his head the crown of life.

This is the kind of honor that goes with this crown.

The Crown of Glory

". . . shepherd the flock of God among you, exercising oversight not under compulsion, but voluntarily, according to the will of God; and not for sordid gain, but with eagerness; nor yet as lording it over those allotted to your charge, but proving to be examples to the flock. And when the Chief Shepherd appears, you will receive the unfading CROWN OF GLORY." (1 Peter 5:2–4 NASB)

It is clear that this is a crown for faithful pastors of the Church. One of the most important spiritual gifts and ministries in the Church is that of pastor-teacher. Those who serve faithfully in this ministry will have a crown and a place of glory forever.

The Crown of Exultation

"For who is our hope or joy or CROWN OF EXULTATION? Is it not even you, in the presence of our LORD Jesus at His coming [in the Rapture]**?"** (1 Thessalonians 2:19 NASB)

This is the soul-winner's crown. Apparently, everyone that we have helped bring to saving faith in the LORD Jesus will be gathered about us in the presence of the LORD at His coming. They will be our joy and crown of exultation. What a fantastic joy it will be to see people (in some cases people you didn't even know) with glorified faces of joy look with thanksgiving to you for helping them see and believe the Gospel.

OUR NEW GARMENTS

Even our clothes will reflect forever our rewards for service in this life:

> **"Let us rejoice and be glad and give the glory to Him, for the marriage of the Lamb has come and His BRIDE [the Church] has made herself ready." And it was given to her to clothe herself in fine linen, bright and clean; for the fine linen is the RIGHTEOUS ACTS of the saints.** (Revelation 19:7–8 NASB)

Apparently there will be distinguishing jewels and embroidery of some sort on our robes to identify righteous deeds of faith.

GOD'S SPECIAL BOOKS

The Book of Tears

"Thou hast taken account of my wanderings;/Put my tears in Thy bottle;/Are they not [all written] IN THY BOOK?" (Psalms 56:8)

In the ancient world of the Middle East, it was common to catch the tears of sorrow and lament in a little flask, and keep them as a remembrance.

As David refers to the wanderings he made while being wrongfully persecuted by King Saul, and all the trials he endured while seeking to follow the LORD, he brings out the following. God has a book in which He records all the tears we suffered while serving Him and seeking to live for Him by faith. I believe that the LORD will reward us a hundredfold for every sorrow we endure for Him.

233

Our LORD is not unfamiliar or unsympathetic with our sorrows and tears. Jesus, who is God, wept at the tomb of His friend Lazarus. He also burst into tears over Jerusalem and the Israelites as He foresaw their rejection of Him as Messiah and the awful consequences that would inevitably come upon them as a result. Our Heavenly Father is full of compassion and understanding.

The Book of Remembrance

The LORD has a book of remembrances in which is recorded all the occasions when we spoke with others about our love and devotion to Him.

Malachi records,

Then those who feared [reverenced] the LORD spoke to one another, and the LORD gave attention and heard it, and a BOOK OF REMEMBRANCE was written before Him for those who fear [reverence] the LORD and who esteem His name. "And they will be Mine," says the LORD of hosts, "on the day that I prepare MY OWN POSSESSION, and I will spare them as a man spares his own son who serves him." (Malachi 3:16–17 NASB)

KINGS AND PRIESTS

The LORD promises that we will be kings and priests forever in His vast kingdom. The Bible says, **"And [Christ] has made us kings and priests unto God and His Father, to Him be glory and dominion forever and ever, Amen."** (Revelation 1:6 KJV)

These very titles suggest something wonderful and exciting. As a non-Christian, I used to think heaven would be a boring place. I thought the only role Christians would have in heaven would be to sit around on clouds and play harps. Not being overly fond of harps, that didn't inspire much enthusiasm in me.

234

But a king rules over someone, and a priest's primary function is to intercede and mediate between some intelligent being and God. This really excites me! It suggests that there may be intelligent beings in other parts of our Heavenly Father's infinite universe where we will serve Him as kings and priests.

HIGHER THAN ANGELS

At present we know that we are lower than angels. The Scriptures say concerning man's present position: **"What is man that Thou rememberest him?/Or the son of man, that Thou art concerned about him?/Thou hast made him for a little while lower than the angels."** (Hebrews 2:6-7 NASB) In this same passage God declares that the world to come has not been subjected to angels, but to redeemed man, who, through the victory won by our representative man and Savior, the Messiah Jesus, will be crowned with glory and honor.

It is mind boggling to think of one day being higher than the angels. The Bible reveals them to be creatures of almost unimaginable power, intelligence, and beauty. Yet the LORD says, **"Do you not know that we will judge angels? How much more the things of this life!"** (1 Corinthians 6:3)

WE SHALL KNOW GOD AS HE NOW KNOWS US

One of the most exciting prospects to me is that heaven is not a static place. We will constantly be learning about the endless, manifold facets of His infinite being.

The Scriptures reveal: **"For now we see in a mirror dimly [obscurely], but then face to face; now I know in part, but then I shall know fully just as I also have been fully known."** (1 Corinthians 13:12 NASB) Mirrors in that day were made of highly polished brass. No matter how fine they were, they had imperfections that caused the reflected image to be slightly obscure and distorted. This is what Paul is conveying about our present ability to know about God. But praise Jesus, we will know Him face to face, and be consumed for all eternity with learning of His resplendent perfections of character.

HOPE, THE KEY TO A DYNAMIC PRESENT FAITH

As we draw ever nearer to that most exciting of all moments, when our LORD Jesus, the Messiah, will suddenly rend the skies, catch us up to meet Him, and transform our mortal bodies into beautiful eternal ones fit for the Father's presence, let us keep feeding our hope with constant reflection upon what God has promised.

"For in hope [of the things promised for eternity] **we have been saved, but hope that is seen is not hope; for why does one also hope for what he sees? But if we hope for what we do not see, with perseverance we wait eagerly for it."** (Romans 8:24–25 NASB)

May you, dear reader, crack the faith barrier, and become so heavenly minded, you're not bogged down by earthly cares! May I see you at His feet with many crowns and a beautiful gown.

Notes

Chapter One
1. John Dart, "Skepticism of Many New Testament Scholars Clashes with Layman's Faith in Traditional Beliefs on Jesus," *Los Angeles Times*, April 27, 1985.
2. For detailed information on the New Age Movement, I recommend: Constance Cumby, *The Hidden Dangers of the Rainbow* (Shreveport, LA: Huntington House, 1983); Caryl Matrisciana, *Gods of the New Age* (Eugene, Oreg.: Harvest House Publishers, 1985); Dave Hunt, *Peace, Prosperity and the Coming Holocaust* (Eugene, Oreg.: Harvest House Publishers, 1983).
3. John Dunphy, "A Religion for a New Age," *Humanist* magazine, January/February 1983, pages 23–26.
4. Jack Canfield and Paula Klimek, "Education in the New Age," *New Age magazine*.
5. Ron Miller, "The Meanings of Education," *Humanist* magazine, March/April 1984, pages 14–16.
6. Benjamin Creme, "The Reappearance of the Christ and The Masters of Wisdom." (North Hollywood, CA: Tara Center Press, 1980).
7. Alice A. Bailey, *The Externalization of the Hierarchy* (Lucis Publishing, 1957), page 548.
8. *Christian Inquirer*, January 1985.
9. *Christian Inquirer*, January 1985.

Chapter Fourteen
1. See chapter four of Hal Lindsey, *Satan Is Alive and Well on Planet Earth* (New York: Bantam Books, 1972).
2. Lindsey, ibid.

Chapter Fifteen

1. On this whole vital subject, I urge everyone to read: Dave Hunt, *The Seduction of Christianity* (Eugene Oreg.: Harvest House Publishers, 1985).

Chapter Sixteen

1. Hal Lindsey, *The Late Great Plant Earth* (New York: Bantam Books, 1973).

ABOUT THE AUTHOR

HAL LINDSEY, named *the bestselling author of the decade* by the New York Times, was born in Houston, Texas. His first book, *The Late Great Planet Earth*, published in 1970, became the bestselling non-fiction book of the decade, selling more than 18 million copies worldwide. He is one of the few authors to have three books on the New York Times bestseller list at the same time.

Mr. Lindsey was educated at the University of Houston. After serving in the U.S. Coast Guard during the Korean War, Mr. Lindsey graduated from Dallas Theological Seminary where he majored in the New Testament and early Greek literature. After completing seminary, Mr. Lindsey served for eight years on the staff of Campus Crusade for Christ, speaking to tens of thousands of students on major university campuses throughout the United States.

Mr. Lindsey currently has an extensive ministry. He is senior pastor of the Palos Verdes Community Church, has a weekly radio talk show heard in over 200 cities, and a regular television show on Trinity Broadcasting Network.

Hal Lindsey has an extensive collection of messages on tape. He has taught many books of the Bible in verse by verse series, as well as prophetic lectures on current world events and issues. If you would be interested in receiving a tape catalogue, please write to the address listed below.

Hal Lindsey Tapes
P.O. Box 4000
Palos Verdes, CA 90274